The
Race
to
Nome

RUSH SERUM BY AIR TO SAVE ALASKANS

SPEED 192 MILES

Alaska, Jan. 31
ome, hemmed
aks and deeply c
to be saved tod
of a diphtheria
town townsmen.

ew Fear Grips Nome

ue City Awaits in Terror Outcome of Test of Frozen
Serum—Officials

eam Was Due at
Miles From Ne-
Midnight.

OME, Alaska — New te
k at plague-ridden N
day.
umors were circulated in
o that the precious se
ed across the icy tundra
teams had been rendered
by freezing.
hed across the icy
s had been

ANTITOXIN, THAWED, RELIEVES NOME DIPTHERIA SUFFERERS

Nome, Alaska, Feb. 3.—The
diphtheria epidemic, which made
Nome desperate for a week while
the town visual-
ized the dra-
matic overland
rush of men
and dogs with
antitoxin from
anchorage, is
believed broken.
There have
been no further
deaths, no new
suspect cases,
and Dr. Curtis
Welch, govern-
ment physician,
who is without
other medical aid in fighting the
scourge, feels confident that the
serum already administered to

Dr. Curtis Welch

ave Trip
ntitoxin Found
fective.

Alaska, Jan. 29 (Asso-
e third relay dog team,
a anti-toxin for Nome
eninsula, was due in
from Nenana
betwee
accordi

was
death
ht. In
na arriv
na, and
ird team
Yukon R
ng in th
e over
Alaska
386

UTHORIZES FLIER TO MAKE NOME DASH

shington Requests Aviator in
irbanks to Carry Antitoxin
to the Stricken City.

SERUM RELIEF NEA FOR STRICKEN NO MAY HAVE ARRI

Seppalla, Champion Dog
Was Due There Yes
After Grueling Da

PLANE

DEATH RACE

5 CENT& SUNDAY 10 CENTS.

TEAMS

Is Expect
and Contin
idemic Ga

al to The Ne
GTON, Ja

i TEAMS WIN RACE TO CARRY SERUM TO N

Into Stricken Alas
Diphtheria Anti-To
Battle With Blizz

the
suspects con
akes his round
Afflicted
rrow quie

FINAL DASH BRINGS ANTITOXIN TO NOME, BUT IT IS FROZEN

Dog Team Starts to Stricken Nome With Anti-toxin

Second Musher Speeds East
to Meet Sled Driver
From Nenana.

e Trails of
by Dog
Hours.

STILL GOOD

Nome Says It
d for Tests—
Forward.

NOM FLIG BEGIN

oy Darling t
Fairbanks T
Pick Up Se

BY ROY S
War Flyer
ment of J
Exclusi
onal News
RANK

E RECORD JOURN
OVER SNO

A BREAKTHROUGH
BOOK

The Race to Nome

*The story of the heroic Alaskan dog
teams that rushed diphtheria serum to
stricken Nome in 1925*

Kenneth A. Ungermann

Edited by Walter Lord

ILLUSTRATED WITH 25 PHOTOGRAPHS

HARPER & ROW, PUBLISHERS
New York, Evanston, and London

To J. B. U.

*"They also serve who only stand
and wait."*

—John Milton, *Sonnet XV*

CONTENTS

ILLUSTRATIONS

PREFACE

During my preliminary research of the 1925 Nenana-to-Nome serum race, I found many of the news accounts written during and shortly after the event distorted or contradictory, largely due to the inaccessibility of the locale of the historic mercy mission. Recording the episode at the time was further complicated by the distance the great race covered. Each of the twenty mushers knew but a few of the other drivers, so there was no one with a comprehensive picture of the 674-mile drive from start to finish.

Later magazine articles, although often well and conscientiously written, apparently were based on the early news stories of the event, for discrepancies continued to appear in print.

It became apparent that much of the basic information in this book would have to come from the actual participants, their survivors, and old-timers who were in Nome during the 1925 diphtheria epidemic.

With this in mind, I flew to Nome and talked with most of the old-timers who had been there in the winter of 1925. The *Nome Nugget* newspaper morgue and many of the local records had been destroyed in a fire that razed Nome in 1934, but I was able to find duplicates at the capital in Juneau.

During the summer, I flew from Nenana down the Tanana and Yukon rivers in my light plane, stopping at the native villages that were transfer points on the serum drive. I was able to find and talk to four of the five surviving drivers of this section of the run, as well as friends and relatives of the drivers who had died. Because of the time which had elapsed since the event, there was confusion about which portion of the trail along the Tanana and Yukon each of the thirteen mushers had driven. But with the help of the surviving drivers I was able to reconstruct the sequence and section that each team covered.

I also flew the route from Unalakleet north and west to Nome and talked with or corresponded with all of the living drivers who traveled the Bering Sea section of the great drive.

I would like to thank participating mushers Sam Joseph, Charlie Olson, Myles Gonangnan, Edgar Nollner, Bill McCarty, Charles Evans, and Harry Pitka for their assistance in outlining the famous drive. Mrs. Gunnar Kaasen, the widow of the finishing driver, contributed to my understanding of her husband's part in the race.

I would like particularly to thank Lula Welch, the widow of Nome's only doctor during the epidemic, for her generous help in outlining the course of the epidemic, substantiated by records in her possession; and later for her careful checking of chapters of the manuscript on Nome for inaccuracies.

Mrs. Carrie McLain is another wonderful woman to whom I am deeply indebted for help. A resident of Nome for many years, Mrs. McLain taught school in remote settlements of northern Alaska for many years after the gold rush. As an ardent historian of "the old days," she was able to furnish me with much valuable material and was a veritable Sherlock Holmes in locating principals in the event who had moved away from Nome.

The biography of Leonhard Seppala, *Seppala, Alaskan Dog Driver*, by Elizabeth Ricker, was valuable background on the famous musher. Mr. Seppala himself furnished useful material on the event, although I could not wholly accept his interpretation of the relative importance of the roles played by several teams in the dramatic story.

Mr. Harold J. Keating of Merck, Sharp, and Dohme, the successors to the manufacturer of the serum used in the Nome epidemic, was good enough to obtain for me photostatic copies of accounts of the event that appeared in eastern newspapers. Miss Irene Griffith, Anchorage librarian, was most helpful in locating reference material for me.

I wish also to express heartfelt thanks to other friends in Nome and elsewhere who played a vital part in the reconstruction of this historic event.

K. U.

The
Race
to
Nome

I A CRY FOR HELP

Dr. Curtis Welch was worried. He listened absently as the wind off the frozen Bering Sea buffeted the house in gusts and made a strumming noise under the eaves. During the afternoon he had been aware of a growing sense of foreboding. Now it had become almost a warning, a premonition of impending disaster.

At first Dr. Welch tried to shake off his anxiety as groundless. But then, he reminded himself, as a physician he had been taught to think analytically. He looked thoughtfully across the living room at his wife and ran his fingers through his tousled gray hair. He searched back over the events of the day, hoping to discover and define the cause of his disquiet.

The time was mid-January, 1925. The day had passed like hundreds before it for Curtis Welch, Nome's only doctor. An Alaskan small-town doctor's days were filled with births and deaths, sickness and recovery, and injuries to be mended. But on this day there had been two unusual cases among the doctor's routine duties: two sick Eskimo children whose illness he had been unable to diagnose. These two exceptions would soon spark a dramatic episode, a life-or-death struggle making Nome the focus of world attention and Dr. Welch's name a byword of courage.

Nome, by 1925, had become very much like an aging movie star: There was still an aura of glamor about the name, but little to sustain it. The turn-of-the-century gold rush, with some twenty thousand hopeful prospectors jostling their way along Front Street, had ended more than fifteen years before. Tents and shacks that had spread out for thirty miles along the "golden sands" during the stampede had long since rotted away. The last major gold strike in the Nome area had taken place in 1904, when deposits were found along the base of the hills which had been a prehistoric beach line of the Bering Sea. After that, gold mining in and around Nome settled down to sedentary routine. The big mining companies with multi-million-dollar dredges moved in to recover the gold deep in the ground, and the days of bonanza pay were over for the lone prospector. The booming, boisterous gold-rush camp had become a small, law-abiding town of 1,429 people—974 whites and 455 Eskimos and half-breeds.

Although Nome had atrophied and shriveled in size, the small settlement remained the most important town on the Seward Peninsula, a vast area of land jutting into the Bering Sea, with its westernmost tip fifty miles from Russian Siberia. A few of the stampeders who had arrived during the early, hectic 1900s stayed on to make Nome their home. The peace of space and solitude kept some; a few had no other home. Most of the Alaskan pioneers, known as "sourdoughs," the backbone of Nome's white population, had married, and their children and Eskimo youngsters filled the white and native schools. Many of the men worked for the big gold-mining companies; others tended store or worked

This picture of Front Street in August, 1900, shows what Nome was like at the height of the gold rush. The town had great difficulty providing adequate housing and supplies for its 10,000 inhabitants. The problems were aggravated by

20,000 other people who did not live in the town itself but came to Nome to socialize, buy provisions, and pick up their mail. In the muddy street before the post office there were often double lines four blocks long.

When the above photograph was taken, in the summer of 1903, hundreds of men had set up temporary quarters on the Sand Spit

modest claims during the short summer months.

In addition to Nome's permanent population, Eskimos from villages dotting the coast lines of Norton Sound and the Bering Sea for hundreds of miles traveled to Nome for supplies and for medical aid. The settlement also served as a shipping point for their furs. Nome's twenty-five-bed May-

west of Nome while trying their luck as gold prospectors. Shacks and tents like these stretched for thirty miles along the coast.

nard-Columbus Hospital, under Dr. Welch's supervision, was the only hospital in trackless northwestern Alaska. Perhaps as many as ten thousand human beings looked to Nome as their closest beacon of civilization.

This particular morning in mid-January, 1925, had held nothing out of the ordinary for Dr.

Welch. Head Nurse Emily Morgan greeted him as he entered the two-story clapboard hospital at 8 A.M. They chatted briefly in low voices and then walked down the main corridor to the ward to begin the doctor's morning rounds. Nurse Morgan stood nearly a head taller than the doctor, who was a slight, short man. Like many large women, she was good-natured and calm. No one could remember seeing her out of sorts. The doctor was habitually cheerful and rather quick in his movements. His speech still reflected his Connecticut background. He had the prematurely worn face of a man solely responsible for many lives (there were no consulting specialists available to Dr. Welch). But that mid-January morning there were no unusual cases at the hospital to alert him against a mass killer that was now hiding in a shack on the outskirts of town.

Later in the morning Nurse Bertha Seville went with the doctor on his house calls. She had been head nurse at the Nome hospital for eight years and was soon going "outside" (to any of the forty-eight states) for a well-earned vacation. Nurse Morgan had been sent to replace her. Bertha Seville had worked with the doctor for so long she seemed to know his very thoughts. She had had much experience with the Eskimos and understood their way of life and their lack of immunity to the white-man's diseases. They trusted her implicitly. Although she was rather plain, a friend described her as "a wonderful woman whose face revealed a devoted nature and bright mind."

After his house calls had been completed, Dr. Welch had returned to his office in the Merchants and Miners Bank of Alaska to cope with the unending paper work connected with his additional duties as director of the U.S. Public Health Service in Nome.

A native man had come to his office during the afternoon and asked him to come quickly, as there were two Eskimo children who were very sick. Dr. Welch had gone at once, walking, since the snow had been light that winter, and he felt he could make better time covering the mile and a half on foot than by waiting for a dog team to be harnessed.

The Sand Spit was an Eskimo settlement west of the Snake River on the fringe of town. The Eskimos around Nome had given up their traditional sod igloos and had copied the white man in house

BROWN BROTHERS

When the gold rush ended and the prospectors left the Sand Spit, Eskimos gave up the sod igloos where they lived in the summer and moved into the abandoned shacks (top). In 1925 they were still building their homes of driftwood and flattened tin cans. Drafty, overcrowded dwellings like the one shown below invited disease, and it was here that the diphtheria epidemic began.

UNDERWOOD & UNDERWOOD

building. Unfortunately what often passed for a house was a miserable shack. Scrap lumber, flattened tin cans, and driftwood were frequently the sole building materials. The houses for the most part were cold, drafty, and overcrowded. Infectious diseases often spread like a wind-driven tundra fire throughout an entire family.

Dr. Welch entered a small, dimly lit house. An Eskimo woman led him to a bed where two very small children lay. He took the pulse of the elder, a child about three. The pulse was light and very rapid. The child's temperature was dangerously high and his breathing labored and shallow. The other child, an infant of one year, had the same symptoms. Dr. Welch shook his head sadly; they were far gone. He doubted if they could be helped.

He asked the mother to tell him when the children had become ill and what their symptoms had been. She replied that they had been sick for three days. She thought it had been a bad cold, for their throats became very sore. Dr. Welch tried to examine their throats, but they would not, or could not, open their mouths far enough for him to see clearly. He comforted the mother, told her he would be back, and left.

By 1925 Nome had become the small, quiet town of 1,429 people shown in these photographs. The bottom picture is a view from Sesnon's Docks. Nome remained practically unchanged until 1934, when fire razed a great portion of the town.

As the doctor walked back to his office he mentally listed conceivable diseases and then discarded them one by one when they did not fit the symptoms. He wished, as he often did, that a good laboratory were available to him, where he could send specimens or a swab for analysis. At one point diphtheria occurred to him—the symptoms were there—but it was highly unlikely. He hadn't seen a case of diphtheria in twenty years in northern Alaska, and it was a contagious disease that required a carrier. He finally dismissed the possibility of diphtheria. No, he thought, Nome had been isolated since the sea had frozen over in the late fall.

Only 140 miles south of the Arctic Circle, Nome was still a remote, isolated frontier outpost. In the fall of the year, after the first film ice congealed over the Bering Sea and the last ship of the season had steamed southward, Nome's only means of transportation to the outside was by dog team. Messages could be sent to other Alaskan towns and to the States through the Army Signal Corps' network of wireless and telegraph stations throughout the Territory, but mail and occasional passengers to or from Nome were carried by relays of dog teams across nearly seven hundred miles of frozen dog trail between Nenana and Nome. For two-thirds of the way the mail trail followed the westward-flowing Tanana and Yukon rivers. The airplane had not yet displaced the sled dog in Alaska.

The valiant mail drivers and their teams of huskies covered the entire distance in all kinds of weather in just under a month. They traveled twenty-five to thirty miles a day, spending each night in shelter cabins or native villages along the trail, where they warmed themselves and fed the dogs. At mail stations, 100 to 150 miles apart, each driver exchanged mail with a musher and team who had been traveling in the opposite direction. After the exchange they returned over their same section of the trail, once again repeating the procedure at the far ends of their routes. In this manner, mail was sent and received weekly in Nome and in Nenana, the closest point to Nome on the Alaska Railroad. From there, mail to the States was carried by train to Seward, an ice-free seaport in south-central Alaska.

As Dr. Welch sat in his home listening to the wind and thinking back over the day, the reason for his sense of foreboding came to him: It was the mysteriously sick Eskimo children on the Sand Spit. He spoke quietly to his wife. "Lula, I've been thinking about those two Eskimo children on the Sand Spit. It's very strange. Children don't die of sore throats or tonsillitis, but they *are* dying, and that's all I could find."

Mrs. Welch, a registered nurse who had married the doctor right after his internship in Los Angeles, gave him a sympathetic look. "I know how difficult it is for you, dear, working without the scientific tools available to most doctors." Kentucky-born Lula Welch knew this better than anyone else; she had worked with the doctor for eighteen years in Alaska.

Despite the doctor's efforts, the two Eskimo children died the following day.

A few days later, on Wednesday, January 21, 1925, Dr. Welch was summoned to the Stanley home to examine a six-year-old boy. Mrs. Stanley told the doctor that Richard had been sick for two days with a sore throat. She had not called the doctor in the beginning because she thought it was only a cold, but the boy had grown rapidly worse. Now she was afraid it might be something else.

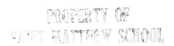

Dr. Welch asked the little boy to open his mouth, and when he had depressed Richard's tongue, he saw and recognized immediately what he had feared to find—the unmistakable dirty white patches of the diphtheria membrane.

The doctor fully realized the terrible implications of his diagnosis. He had on hand 75,000 units of antitoxin. It was enough for only a few inoculations, and since it was five years old, it might have lost its effectiveness. Diphtheria, unless checked, would spread with devastating speed. Only last summer he had asked the Seattle regional office of the U.S. Public Health Service for additional serum, but none had been sent. Now it was too late.

In a small snow-and-ice-bound town like Nome everyone knew everyone else, and visiting was the most popular way of alleviating the boredom of the long winter days. How many people had been exposed or infected already? He would soon know. The incubation period was less than a week.

Dr. Welch told Mrs. Stanley his findings. He instructed her to permit no one in the house and to keep her other children at home. The doctor returned to his home before going to the hospital to pick up antitoxin for Richard Stanley. But the little boy was not to live through the night.

Dr. Welch burst into the kitchen where his wife was preparing lunch.

"Lu," he said, "we are faced with a diphtheria epidemic. Call Mayor Maynard and have him convene the City Council at once. We must establish a quarantine, close the schools and movie house, and take every precaution to check the spread of the disease. Above all, we must find some way to get antitoxin to Nome within two weeks."

George Maynard, mayor and publisher of the newspaper, the *Nome Nugget,* listened with deepening concern as Dr. Welch explained clearly the gravity of the situation. The mayor and the City Council acted quickly on the doctor's recommendation to create a board of health to enforce quarantine and handle the mechanics of combatting an epidemic. Mr. M. L. Summers, superintendent of the Hammon Consolidated Gold Fields, was named chairman and empowered to form a board to help him carry out his instructions.

Dr. Welch said, "Gentlemen, antitoxin will check the spread of this virulent disease and help save those who have been infected. We must have serum. If we have to wait for antitoxin to be shipped from Seattle, it may not get here in time to do us much good. Even if we find some serum in Alaska," he added, "we still must then find a way to get it to Nome before the epidemic is out of hand."

Mayor Maynard suggested that if serum were located in Alaska, perhaps a daring pilot could fly it from Fairbanks to Nome. This possibility was discussed, but the others present thought it was doubtful an airplane could make it through to Nome in the cold winter of 1925. Alaskan bush flying was in its infancy and the few planes in the Territory were unreliable, open, and limited to summer flying because of weather conditions. No one knew for certain whether a plane would operate at forty to sixty degrees below zero, or whether a pilot in an open plane could keep from freezing at these temperatures.

Someone in the room finally said, "We know dog teams can make it through. If we find serum, it can be sent to Nenana by rail. We could send a team to the rail line, or we can radio Nenana and ask them to pick a fast team and start the antitoxin down the Tanana and Yukon rivers. Then we can

Eskimo women and children of Nome's Sand Spit district posed for these pictures shortly before the 1919 flu epidemic. The flu took a heavy toll of white families, but among the Eskimos, who had built up no immunity to white-men's diseases, the epidemic was even worse. Entire villages were wiped out. The same thing had happened in 1900, when two sailors came to Alaska with measles, which decimated the Eskimo population. Welch realized in 1925 that unless antitoxin was obtained quickly, hundreds of women and children like these would die.

have one of our best teams from here meet it halfway, somewhere around Nulato. Perhaps we can
cut the mail time in half and get it to Nome in fifteen days."

None of the responsible men in the room had to
be reminded of the additional and terrible threat of
an epidemic in an area where the population was
predominantly Eskimo. The native population had
built up little or no immunity to the white-man's
diseases. The 1919 influenza epidemic had wiped
out entire Eskimo villages. Even in Nome, where
medical care was available, the epidemic had left
ninety-one "flu orphans."

Dr. Welch told the mayor and the council, "The
first thing we must do is send a wireless message to
other Alaskan cities, telling them of our situation
and our urgent need for antitoxin."

The mayor and the City Council instructed Dr.
Welch to compose and send a message immediately. He quickly wrote the message and took it to
Sergeant James Anderson, who was in charge of
the U.S. Army Signal Corps radiotelegraph station
in Nome. The sergeant silently read the radiogram
and looked inquiringly at Dr. Welch.

"Send this as a priority message to Juneau, Fairbanks, and Seward," Dr. Welch instructed him.

"Doc," Anderson said, "I guess we had better go on twenty-four-hour duty here. I'll tell the other boys."

The sergeant called Privates Joe Durand, C. T. Selestrom, and Joseph Monis and told them the bad news.

In seconds Dr. Welch's message was flashing across frozen tundra, virgin forests, and mighty mountains sheathed with ageless glaciers. His simple words telling of Nome's plight would soon focus the attention of the entire nation upon the Bering Sea community.

11 THE MAIL TRAIL

As Dr. Welch gravely faced the City Council in Nome twenty other men—scattered across hundreds of miles of desolate, snow-covered tundra of the Bering Sea littoral and the frozen, forested valleys of the Yukon and Tanana rivers of central Alaska—went about their daily chores. These simple, indomitable men and their courageous sled dogs would soon take part in an epic struggle against death.

Racially they were a diverse group: Eskimo, Russian-Eskimo, Norwegian, Irish, half-breed Indian, and pure-blooded Koyukuk and Yukon Indian—branches of the great Athabascan tribe that stretches across Canada and is related to the Navajos of Arizona and New Mexico. But these men had certain qualities in common. Foremost were a stamina and toughness almost beyond the comprehension of men in cities and towns. They knew how to work and survive during the long, subzero winters of northern Alaska. Perhaps most important for what was to come, they had an understanding and working partnership with the sled dogs of the North.

It would be false to say these men loved their dogs as pets. Rather it was a case of mutual respect. The man depended on the sled dog for his winter livelihood; with a small team he worked his trap line—twenty miles or more long—picking up fur and resetting the traps. His dogs helped him bring in his moose or caribou kill during the long, cold, hungry months. Not infrequently his dog team performed an urgent mission of mercy, carrying a critically ill or injured person to the nearest nurse or doctor.

Along the Bering Sea coast, men used dog teams in the winter for hauling freight to outlying gold camps. During the summer, transporting supplies over the spongy tundra would be impossible in many areas.

All of the men who owned their own teams had at least one dog who was more than a beast of burden. This was the lead dog. He had been carefully selected or, rather, had shown attributes that had set him apart from and above the other dogs. These traits of leadership were not always easily discernible, nor was each of the traits common to all lead dogs. Some leaders had remarkable trail sense; they could follow a trail heavily drifted over, their sense of direction seemingly infallible. Others had a facility for understanding their masters' words and wishes, coupled with unswerving obedience. Still others seemed to have an indefinable essence of leadership, a magnetic influence over the other dogs that made them willing followers.

Contrary to legend, lead dogs do not become leaders through a free-for-all of guttural snarls and slashing teeth from which the leader emerges victorious. Some of the best leaders are relatively small dogs who, when possible, avoid conflict. Good lead dogs, however, have one essential trait: They are above average in canine intelligence.

These lead dogs, the aristocracy of the sled-dog

world, occupied a special niche in the hearts and esteem of their masters. It was not a fawning, petting relationship. More often than not a mutual, deep affection and regard existed between master and dog. These leaders and their teammates were work dogs who had made possible the opening of the Alaskan frontier.

Over 650 miles from Nome, near the extreme eastern end of the mail trail to Nenana, a dog team threaded its way along the east bank of the Tanana River. A young white man stood on the wooden runners at the rear of the sled and gripped the two handles that were curved extensions of the nearly vertical uprights enclosing the back of the long freight and mail sled. The handles, very much like plow handles, helped the driver turn the sled in heavy snow and on sharp turns. On the lighter racing sleds the driver gripped a horizontal crosspiece.

From time to time the driver would shift his weight to his right foot and push with his left in the same manner a child pushes a scooter. The man wore the native fur parka—a hip-length fur jacket with a hood enveloping his head. The hood was bordered with a wolverine fur fringe that extended beyond his face. Wolverine fur shed ice that formed from breath more easily than other furs.

The young man, a mail musher, was pushing the sled for two reasons: It helped him keep warm, as it was 46° below zero—not exceptionally cold for north of the Alaska Range—and it helped his tired dogs over the slight rises of the Tanana Valley. He was careful to breathe through his nose; a deep breath through the mouth, even at −46°, could freeze his lungs.

During the afternoon the temperature had been falling. There was not a whisper of wind and the clear air had a heavy, almost solid feeling. The driver knew from experience these conditions often prefaced a period of extreme cold.

That night, Wednesday, January 21, fifty miles northeast of the mail team, the mercury in the U.S. Weather Bureau thermometer at Fairbanks would sink to −57°. Nenana, the driver's destination, a short distance to the south, would record 62° below zero before morning.

The Weather Bureau described the cold weather phenomenon as a continental arctic high-pressure system. During the long winter nights of the sub-arctic, the surface warmth of the earth radiated outward and the short hours of daylight, with the sun barely rising above the horizon, gave back to the earth little warmth to replace the heat lost by radiational cooling. If there were no competing weather systems from warmer areas to mix with and warm the supercooled atmosphere, a great cold, and therefore heavy, air mass would form and sink to earth, displacing the belt of warmer surface air.

Strangely, the coldest points, or "cold poles," in the northern hemisphere are not located in the arctic, but in the subarctic. One is in Siberia near Verkhoyansk; the other is in the Yukon Basin of east-central Alaska and Canada's Yukon Territory. A record low of $-84°$ was reported at Snag, along the Alaskan-Canadian border.

Men who work and survive in the Far North recognize the extreme cold as a formidable and potentially lethal adversary. In temperatures down to $-50°$, a properly dressed man can perform his work without too much discomfort or danger. Below $-50°$, survival becomes a grim battle.

Sled dogs often refuse to travel, knowing instinctively that nature's evolutionary adaptation has not equipped them for such temperatures. In the open, huskies tramp a bowl-like nest in the snow

In 1925 the Yukon River was a large part of the mail route between Nome and Nenana, for boats in summer and sleds in winter.

and curl up with their bushy tails over their noses to protect their lungs from the heavy, biting cold.

U.S. Mail mushers, who drive their dogs regardless of extreme temperatures, keep the teams going at a slow pace to prevent heavy breathing or panting and subsequent "lung scorching."

A man in temperatures below −50° feels oppressed, as if mentally and physically he were being pushed down by a great weight. His movements become slow and laborious. Many men of the North grow beards to protect their faces from the cold, but moisture from their breath clings and freezes

The mail drivers of the Northern Commercial Company looked very much like this man and his dog team on a frozen Alaskan river.

to the individual face hairs. Soon their lower faces become matted with an icy crust of rime.

At abnormally low temperatures a man familiar with the hazards of cold moves slowly and deliberately, except for occasionally stamping his feet and briskly beating his arms to restore circulation. A minor trail accident could be quickly fatal. A broken leg that prevented a man from gathering wood for a fire could mean his death in a few hours.

In Canada's Yukon Territory a law was enacted forbidding the proprietor of a roadhouse (inn) or other hostelry to lock his doors at night from autumn to spring. Travelers had frozen to death while beating on a locked door to awaken the sleeping innkeeper.

Of the many cold-weather dangers, mushers fear water above all else. A breakthrough into a snow-camouflaged spring or a hidden overflow can be calamitous at low temperatures. Wet feet freeze in minutes. A quick fire or a change to dry footwear is the only insurance against severe frostbite and amputation. Most drivers carry extra socks and wear Eskimo mukluks, knee-high moccasin-type boots usually made of sealskin and sewn carefully with sinew so that with the drawstring tied beneath the knee, they resist water penetration.

The extreme cold has only one favorable aspect. When from time to time the great arctic air masses seep down over Alaska's interior and send the mercury plunging, the heavy air becomes like a pool of still water. There is not a breath of wind to ripple the crystal-clear atmosphere, and a great silence settles over the land. If the wind blew, neither exposed man nor beast could survive.

Ahead, through the clear, glimmering subarctic twilight, the mail driver could see dark specks against the snow. From long familiarity with the trail he knew these and the flickers of yellow light were the town of Nenana, where he lived. With the fast condition of the trail he would cover the intervening three miles in less than thirty minutes.

It was 3:45 in the afternoon, but the sun had set at 2:55; there were only five hours and forty-five minutes of daylight on January 21 along the sixty-fifth parallel north. (A month earlier, on the shortest day of the year, from sunrise to sunset there were only three hours and forty-two minutes of daylight.) The driver hummed a little tune. He had been on the mail run several days and was looking forward to home, where his wife waited for him. Within a week his name would become famous as the driver of the first leg of the great Nenana-to-Nome serum race.

Three hundred trail miles west of Nenana—almost halfway to Nome—Galena, an Athabascan Indian village, squatted on the north bank of the mighty Yukon River. The Tanana, after absorbing the tributary waters of the Kantishna River, had already converged with the Yukon as it searched its way westward to the Bering Sea. At Galena the great river swelled to a mile in width. Ten miles to the south, the foothills of the treeless, snow-covered Kaiyuk Mountains rose out of the smooth floor of the Yukon Valley. Except for Galena, there was no other sign of life as far as the eye could see.

In Galena a young Indian of medium height stepped out of his house into the dog yard, carrying a basket in his right hand. The copper-skinned man was typical of many Athabascans along hundreds of miles of the Yukon River. Seven large gray dogs were evenly spaced about the small yard. Each dog was curled in a tight ball with its nose tucked under its tail. The dogs' breath rose slowly like white smoke, condensing into minute ice crystals in the still, subzero air. Each dog was chained to a stake, with perhaps a six-foot radius of movement. They were never allowed to run loose; it would destroy their enthusiasm for work. Getting into harness and pulling a sled for them meant relative freedom and an end to the boredom of being tied in one place.

As the first dog spotted his master he lunged against his chain, wagging his bushy tail. Soon the yard was filled with a chorus of howls, resembling those of coyotes or wolves more than the barking of dogs. The bedlam increased as the man threw a chunk of fish to the first dog. The dogs had been worked hard bringing in firewood, and each would receive two or three pounds of dried salmon and a pound of tallow. These sled dogs ranged in weight from sixty to eighty pounds. They had masklike markings over the head, erect ears, and the dark gray of their bodies turned to a gray-white on their faces, setting off their eyes.

The man called his dogs malamutes (pronounced "mal-e-moot"), as did most Indian dog drivers of the interior, although this was not quite technically correct. Early Russian explorers named the dog after an Alaskan Chukchi Sea Eskimo tribe known as Malamutes, who had developed the breed. But the name, by usage, had also come to cover other native Alaskan dogs. "Husky" is a general term covering all types of sled dogs.

The Indian's huskies were strong and rugged. Their wolflike appearance was no accident as they were the descendants of wolves as well as dogs. (Some of the dogs of native teams are as much as one-half wolf. They tend to viciousness, but are known for their stamina.)

On his way back to the house the Indian patted the head of his lead dog. He was very proud of this dog; she had helped him win a number of races.

This musher and his dogs were representative of

other Yukon Indians and their teams up and down the great river's broad valley. These men would soon play an essential part in speeding the desperately needed diphtheria antitoxin toward Nome.

About 160 miles west of Galena the mail trail descends from a range of low mountains and approaches the seemingly endless expanse of the Bering Sea. The trail finally reaches the sea at Unalakleet, an Eskimo village perched on the edge of Norton Sound. Some three hundred natives and a handful of whites live in clustered igloos and cabins in this Bering Sea community. It has not changed perceptibly for many years.

In Unalakleet on Wednesday, January 21, 1925, an Eskimo was lacing new rawhide to his dog sled where some of the old fastenings had broken. A half mile from shore his wife crouched patiently over a hole cut in the sea ice. She alternately lifted and dropped a short stick, attached to a line of finely split whalebone which went down through a hole in the ice. Whalebone was better than the whiteman's fish line as ice did not readily cling to it. She was jigging for tom cod. The fish would be used to feed her family as well as her husband's sled dogs. She seemed impervious to the cold wind blowing across the ice. Through uncounted generations her people had learned to adapt themselves to the forbidding land and climate in which they lived.

Although the arrival of the white man had changed little in their customs, the Alaskan Eskimos' life had become a little easier. At least they no longer faced recurring periods of starvation. The Eskimo wife's parents and grandparents had been forced at times to eat their leather garments at the end of a hard winter, when hunting and fishing had been poor. Now they were given emergency supplies, and reindeer herds had been imported to provide a better supply of meat. Despite their hard life, Eskimos were and are a happy people.

The Bering Sea coastal climate is entirely different from the weather of the interior. Very low winter temperatures are almost unknown, but subzero temperatures, at times accompanied by high winds and snow, combine to make the weather more dangerous than the extreme cold of the interior.

In zero wind conditions the body is surrounded by a layer of radiated heat over the exposed parts, as well as by the heat trapped in layers of clothing. When cold wind blows, the layer of heat is removed and convective cooling, or loss of body heat, takes place, which causes a change of metabolism. Naturally the efficiency of clothing will determine how much wind and cold a man can survive, but recent tests on wind chill of exposed flesh by army arctic research technicians have produced some startling comparative figures. For example, $30°$ above zero with a wind of forty-five miles per hour is equivalent to $-40°$ with a wind of two miles per hour. The rate of cooling at $11°$ above with only a ten-mile-per-hour wind is equivalent to below $-40°$ with no wind.

The Eskimo fixing his sled had never heard of "wind-chill effect," but he knew accurately from experience the effects of various weather combinations. His life depended on the knowledge, and survival techniques had been passed down from father to son for many generations.

Eskimos caught out in sudden blizzards on the trackless tundra of the arctic and subarctic have found a method of survival even without shelter. If there is insufficient snow to build a snow cave, an Eskimo will simply sit cross-legged on the ground with his back to the wind and his head bent almost to his knees. He then goes to sleep. In this way he is presenting the smallest possible area of his body to the chilling wind, and by sleeping he is conserving his body energy and heat.

As time slips by, the cold gradually penetrates his fur garments, and before he freezes to death the discomfort wakens him. (Contrary to popular belief, cold awakens a sleeping person before he freezes.) The Eskimo then gets up and exercises to restore circulation before sitting down and going to sleep again. He will repeat these actions until the blizzard has abated and he can find his way home.

It is questionable whether this survival technique would work as well for the white man; the Eskimo is better able to withstand cold because of his high fat diet and slightly different metabolism.

The Eskimo's knowledge of the treacherous sea ice and coastal storms, which had been shared with white men along the Bering Sea, soon would be decisive in the success or failure of the memorable race against time.

Three Eskimos and their dog teams would take part in the ordeal of cold and blizzard that lay ahead. Without their painfully acquired lore of survival in this harsh, frozen land, the delivery of the vital serum to Nome would have been doomed to failure.

III   300,000 UNITS OF SERUM

Signal Corps operators monitoring short-wave radios in Alaska's scattered towns and small cities heard Sergeant Anderson keying Nome's call signal and immediately responded: "Go ahead, Nome."

The Army-trained technicians painstakingly tuned the dials of their sensitive receivers to record every dot and dash of Dr. Welch's radiotelegraph message speeding across the ether from the Bering Sea village.

Acknowledgments flashed back to Nome from Fairbanks, Anchorage, and Seward. Within minutes the urgent request for help had been relayed to

Juneau, the territorial capital, well over a thousand miles to the southeast of Nome. In each city the message was quickly transcribed from the Morse code broadcast and delivered by messenger to the community's leading officials.

In Juneau Governor Scott Bone frowned as he studied Dr. Welch's plea for help. He seemed lost in concentration for a minute and then turned to an aide.

"This is bad news," he said. "Radio Nome and tell them we will do everything we can to locate antitoxin and get it to them as quickly as possible."

Then Governor Bone passed Dr. Welch's message to another assistant, instructing him to relay it to Alaska's Washington delegate, Dan Sutherland. "Tell Dan to move heaven and earth to enlist immediate Administration help," he added.

Later messages from the stricken city, emphasizing the emergency and indicating the disease was spreading, listed several new cases. The wire services, Associated Press, United Press, and International News Service, were informed of the threatening development in Nome. Newsmen at once sensed a dramatic story—an isolated Alaskan town desperately needed help. Across the na-

By 1925 Front Street had changed from the crowded, ramshackle thoroughfare
of the gold rush days to a placid small-town street, with decent paving and

electricity. Shortly after this picture was taken, the first diphtheria cases broke out, and a general quarantine left the street quite deserted.

tion teletype keys clattered out the story of Nome's crisis. Here and there in American cities newspaper editors tore off the wire-service copy from teletype machines and hurried to their typewriters to write a late bulletin.

As the days passed, news stories on the potential epidemic appeared in the nation's papers with increasing frequency. Once again, growing thousands of Americans were seeing the word "Nome" in print. This time their reaction was sympathy and a wish to help, not envy or lust for the quick gold that had once made Nome famous. Remote Nome was no longer alone. People everywhere stopped and wondered out loud what could be done to halt the "Black Death" in the small ice-bound town.

In Washington, D.C., Alaskan Delegate Dan Sutherland received full cooperation from the U.S. Public Health Service. Perhaps the agency was trying to atone for having failed to stockpile the expensive serum in Nome as a safeguard against such an emergency. With the help of major drug firms Washington officials were able to trace recent West Coast shipments of diphtheria antitoxin. Many of these orders were rerouted to the regional headquarters of the Health Service in Seattle, Washington, and plans for boat shipment of 1,100,000 units to Seward, Alaska, went forward.

There was widespread relief when it was learned that Dr. J. B. Beeson at the Alaska Railroad hospital in Anchorage had recently received and had on hand 300,000 units of the life-saving serum. It was not much, but if it could be sent quickly to Nome, it would stem the tide of the epidemic until an adequate supply of serum arrived. The average victim who had contracted the disease required an inoculation of some 30,000 units to combat the illness, but much could be done with a small amount as immunization. One to three thousand units usually sufficed to prevent the disease in one who had been exposed.

After being informed of the available serum in Anchorage, Governor Bone set the rescue machinery in motion. He carefully considered the only alternatives of getting the serum to Nome: dog teams from the railhead at Nenana versus an airplane from Fairbanks. He ruled unequivocally in favor of dog teams for the first serum shipment.

Fairbanks, with a sense of civic pride in its pioneer aircraft company and an earnest desire to help Nome, bombarded the governor and Delegate

Sutherland with telegrams requesting authorization to carry the serum to Nome by air. The Fairbanks Airplane Company had two open cockpit, Hisso-powered Standard biplanes. They were flown only in the summer and had been dismantled and stored for the winter. Former Navy pilot Roy Darling, an agent in Alaska for the Justice Department, and mechanic Ralph Mackie, a former Royal Canadian Air Force flyer living in Anchorage, volunteered to attempt the flight if one of the planes could be reassembled quickly. Without waiting for official approval, Mr. Rodebaugh, a railroad conductor and head of the Fairbanks Airplane Company, gave orders to have the plane readied for the flight.

The governor's decision to use dog teams for the mercy mission proved to be wiser, however, in the light of later developments. General aviation in 1925 was still suffering intense growing pains, and flying in Alaska was almost unknown. The Wright brothers' first flight at Kitty Hawk had taken place only twenty-two years earlier, and airplanes had not passed beyond the experimental stage until 1914–1918, during World War I. True, five years before, the Army Air Service's Black Wolf Squadron had accomplished its famous four-plane New York-to-Nome flight; and since then, a few courageous flyers, Ben Eilson, Noel Wien, and others had begun to etch their names in the pale northern skies. Nevertheless, what little flying there was in Alaska was limited to the warmer months. It was questionable whether a pilot could survive winter flying in the open cockpit planes then in use.

Governor Bone knew the hazard in attempting to fly the serum through would be twofold: There was a better than even chance that an airplane would not make it through to Nome, with the resultant loss of its crew; and if the plane crashed, the serum would be lost, and with it perhaps Nome's only chance of avoiding a runaway epidemic.

Governor Bone told territorial officials that he felt the existing flying equipment in Alaska was inadequate and that only relatively unskilled flyers were available. But he did not rule out the possibility of using aircraft to carry part of the additional serum being shipped from Seattle.

Once he had made his decision, he quickly gave orders to have it carried out. A territorial official was instructed to contact the Northern Commercial Company to arrange for dog teams along the route.

Northern Commercial, Alaska's much smaller

counterpart of Canada's Hudson's Bay Company, had a far-flung network of trading posts, river steamers, and general stores. This company held the U.S. Mail-delivery contract from Fairbanks down the Tanana and Yukon valleys to Unalakleet. Mushers and dogs of the mail teams were carefully selected. The mail drivers adopted the pony express slogan, "The mail must go through!" And go through it did in all sorts of weather, from November, when the river ice was firm, until "breakup" in late May, when the ice and snow melted and the river steamers took over. During the many winters Star Route (rural) mail was carried by sled in the Alaskan bush country, the Northern Commercial Company was never fined or reprimanded for late delivery of the government mails.

After arranging for a number of mail teams to carry the serum, the governor telegraphed Mr. Wetzler, the U.S. Post Office inspector in Nenana. Governor Bone authorized him to send a message down the Yukon calling additional teams to the trail so that the great race against time could be made in even shorter relays and therefore with greater speed.

In small Signal Corps relay cabins situated at

forty-mile intervals along the winding course of
the Yukon River, a bell rang and the operators received and relayed the terse message from Wetzler:
"Request the best musher and team in your section
to stand by to receive the serum for Nome starting
from Nenana tomorrow."

The word was passed quickly to regular mail
drivers along the route. One of the two Signal
Corps operators manning each station then slipped
into his parka, strapped on snowshoes, and headed
for the nearest native settlement with the news and
to ask for their best dog team and driver. Word of
Nome's plight and the forthcoming race against
death with the serum spread with incredible speed
along the Yukon and up its many tributaries. Word-
of-mouth exchanges, known in Alaska as "mukluk
telegraph," winged the message far from the main
river arteries of the interior. In the Far North, as in
other primitive and vast lands, communication
without mechanical aid was surprisingly swift and
accurate.

Hurried meetings were held in little villages
along the Yukon Valley to select the best drivers
and dogs to send to the mail trail. Often a team was
formed from the individually fastest dogs in a vil-

lage and loaned to the man who was acknowledged to be the best musher. Warmest fur clothes were donned, harness and sleds were checked. And then, when all was ready, the chosen teams drifted out of the birch and alder thickets and the silent spruce stands to the mail shelter cabins along the 450-mile trail to Unalakleet. There they began their vigil, each driver waiting his turn to take the package of serum one step closer to Nome.

As the news swept across the country that diphtheria antitoxin had been located in Alaska and would be carried over hundreds of miles of northern wilderness to Nome by relays of men and dog teams, the brassy blaring of the Jazz Age seemed momentarily silenced. Society capers, divorces, organized crime, and the antics of faddists—all the trivia of a prohibition nation with a war hangover —were diminished in importance for a few days. The imagination of America was gripped by the vision of a man and his dog team fighting stubbornly across a white wilderness against elements whose extremes were almost beyond comprehension. Editorial writers pointed out that men with dogs would attempt this for their fellow men, in the machine age, when no man-made machine could get through. It made people both proud and humble.

Even the international press had begun to report the approaching deadly contest of stamina and speed against time and the northern elements. Within a few days, in London, Paris, Stockholm, and other cities of the world, the unfamiliar names of Nenana, Tolovana, Tanana, Kokrines, Ruby, Whiskey Creek, and Nulato would momentarily escape anonymity as people throughout the literate world traced the swift relay teams down the windings of the frozen Tanana and Yukon rivers.

In Anchorage Dr. Beeson read the telegram from Washington authorizing him to release the 300,000 units of serum and to ship it at once to Nenana. As soon as Dr. Beeson had learned of Nome's desperate need, he anticipated the telegram from the capital giving him permission to ship the serum north and had already started packing the disease-combatting liquid when the message arrived.

The railroad hospital doctor was no stranger to the Alaskan bush country. He fully understood the problems of a winter-locked, remote Alaskan settlement when sickness strikes. A few years before the Nome epidemic, Dr. Beeson had traveled over five hundred miles by dog team relays from Anchorage to the gold-mining camp of Iditarod to the bedside of a critically sick person. To reach Iditarod the physician had had to traverse a high pass of the lofty Alaskan Range, a winter journey the most seasoned mushers were reluctant to undertake.

Dr. Beeson still felt a sense of relief when he recalled a nearly fatal accident that had occurred on that trip. Somewhere near the Kuskokwim River his Indian driver headed the team down a bank of a small slough. Dr. Beeson was tied to the sled to keep from being thrown off, for they were traveling at a brisk speed over rough terrain. As the team reached the middle of the frozen marsh Beeson heard a sharp cracking noise, and the sled plunged with him through shell ice into the cold water of a hidden stream. He tried desperately to untie the ropes binding him to the sled, but he was unable to find the knots. He felt himself submerge in the numbing water and later remembered thinking the end had come. Suddenly he felt the sled lurch and found himself emerging from the stream. Dr. Beeson looked up through the water streaming down his face and saw the dog team struggling up the bank of the slough, still pulling the sled and its sodden cargo.

Anchorage, the starting point of the serum's journey to Nome, is the largest city in Alaska. In the background is the Chugach Range.

The driver, who had jumped clear of the break-through, had a fire going by the time the doctor peeled off his wet, and by then freezing, clothes. He suffered no ill effects from his icy bath, but often thought how lucky he had been.

Dr. Beeson carefully packed the vials containing the 300,000 units of serum into a cylindrical container and wrapped it with a piece of insulating quilting. He then gave orders to have the package covered with tough khaki-colored canvas. When the packing was completed, the compact bundle weighed just twenty pounds. Dr. Beeson knew that pound for pound nothing else in the world could equal the value of this package to the people of Nome. He hoped the careful wrapping would help protect the serum against expected jolts and sub-zero temperatures. He had done all that he could to ensure the safety of the vital liquid.

On Monday, January 26, 1925, Dr. Beeson took the serum to the Anchorage station and handed the package to conductor Frank Knight of the Alaska Railroad. Knight listened attentively to the doctor's admonitions for its care and placed the twenty-pound bundle in a protected corner in the baggage car of the Fairbanks train.

Back on the station platform, Knight looked at

his watch, cried "All-a-board," and hand-signaled forward to the locomotive as he swung onto the steps of a passenger car.

Engineer Charlie Mathieson blew the train's whistle and slowly opened the throttle. Steam locomotive "66" billowed smoke and steam and then chuffed with an increasing tempo as it gathered speed northward to begin the preliminary 298-mile leg of a memorable journey.

IV   THE RACE BEGINS

As the Anchorage-to-Fairbanks Passenger Special rumbled up the broad Susitna Valley, in a kennel on the outskirts of Nome a big black husky got
up and stretched. He was one of some thirty-odd
sled dogs belonging to Leonhard Seppala of the Pioneer Mining Company, or rather the Hammon
Consolidated Gold Fields. Consolidated had recently bought out the founding company, though
most people continued to call it by its original
name. The mining company fed the renowned racing musher's huskies in return for their use as company sled dogs.

The black dog's name was Balto, and his kennel boss, Leonhard Seppala, considered him only a fair dog—a good enough freighter, but without any outstanding characteristics and certainly lacking sufficient speed to make one of Seppala's famous racing teams.

Balto seemed unconcerned over his master's lack of approbation, and in the winter went his calm way as a team member, hauling freight to the company's widely scattered placer mines. From time to time in the summer Balto and some of the other dogs were hitched to a small flatcar of the abandoned Nome-Kougarok narrow-gauge railway. They pulled the flatcar, which served as a bus for the miners, to and from the mines a few miles out of town. Seppala called the unusual conveyance a pupmobile.

As Balto ended his luxurious stretch he looked thoughtfully for a moment to the east and then raised his nose and gave a long, sad, wolflike howl. But of course Balto had no way of knowing that a khaki-colored package in the baggage car of a train nearly a thousand miles to the southeast would, within a week, make him the most famous dog in the world.

In another part of the kennel a smallish, light gray dog with erect ears and alert, pale blue eyes thumped his tail as he heard the door of his kennel open. The little forty-eight-pound Siberian husky called Togo was, if not the most famous dog in the world, certainly the most famous lead dog in Alaska at that time. Togo had been named for the tough little Japanese admiral who soundly defeated the Russian Navy at Port Arthur, Manchuria, in 1904. He had lived up to his name; as Seppala's lead dog he had won every important race in Alaska.

The shadow of an impending event was also being cast across Togo's future. But now, like Balto, he was unaware that in a few days he, too, would play a vital role in bringing the serum one step closer to Nome. The twelve-year-old dog could not know the grueling drive would be his last great race before a well-earned retirement.

Togo did understand, however, that something important was about to happen. For the past few days his master had hitched Togo and his fastest teammates to the sled every day and had driven them on the trails around Nome. Togo knew from long experience that daily runs like this prefaced

At the time of the epidemic, Leonhard Seppala was the finest dog sled driver in Alaska and the winner of the All-Alaskan Sweepstakes for three consecutive years. In 1925, at the age of 48, he was still in his prime. This picture of Seppala and Togo was taken after one of their many racing victories.

a race. During the training period all of Seppala's dogs showed their eagerness in the hope that they would be selected for the final starting team.

After it had become apparent dog teams would be the most logical choice for transporting the serum, Mr. Summers, Seppala's boss and also the chairman of the Board of Health, had gone to Seppala and asked him if he could go all the way to Nenana and bring the serum back to Nome. He told the musher that the Board of Health felt Seppala should be the one to make the trip, as his was the fastest team and he was acknowledged one of the best dog drivers in the Territory.

Summers later told Seppala that Nenana had been asked to pick a fast team and to have it carry the serum halfway to meet Seppala at Nulato on the Yukon. Summers added that there was still some hope that an airplane could carry it through to Nome, but until a final decision was made, Seppala must be ready to leave at a moment's notice.

Seppala replied that if the board had confidence in him, he would make the trip. Although his racing team was in good physical condition, the snow had been light that winter and he had not used them as much as usual. He told Summers that he would start exercising and hardening his dogs at once for the long three-hundred-mile drive and that he planned to take two teams. He would start out with twenty dogs and drop twelve at road-houses and Eskimo igloos on the way so that on the return trip he could exchange tired or foot-injured dogs for fresh ones. Seppala said in this way he could run the antitoxin day and night and return to Nome in the shortest possible time.

For a few days, until the governor made his final decision on sending the serum by dog team and until the train reached Nenana, Seppala and his famous "Siberian Rats" were seen daily, running along the slopes of the low hills behind Nome or threading their way—appearing from a distance like a black reptile—among the ice hummocks and pressure ridges of the Bering Sea.

Aboard the Fairbanks-bound train the hours passed. Glowing warmly in the early darkness of Tuesday, January 27, the railroad section-house lights of Broad Pass, Summit, and Cantwell slipped by as the train wound its way slowly upward and then down through tortuous Windy Pass in the Alaska Range.

As the train had climbed into higher country,

snowbanks on each side of the track increased in depth. From time to time the train slowed and blew its whistle angrily. Old hands in the passenger cars knew that another moose was on the tracks. Sometimes the moose would struggle off into the deep snow at the train's whistle, but often it would amble on down the tracks ahead of the train until the engineer lost patience.

Later a section crew with a handcar would go along the tracks to salvage the moose meat for shipment to Anchorage and Fairbanks for the native hospitals and orphanages.

Fifty miles to the west, 20,320-foot Mt. McKinley was outlined with a luminous pink glow as the continent's highest mountain caught the last rays of the sun, now far below the horizon. Nenana was but a few hours away.

"Wild Bill" Shannon looked impatiently at his watch. He had already been out two separate times to check the harness and the tied dogs and was now anxious to begin the run to Tolovana. The night was clear and star-filled. The temperature hovered just above $-40°$. The young mail driver was thankful that the weather had warmed a little. The night before, the mercury had fallen to $53°$ below zero—too cold to make good time.

Shannon looked down the street at the lights in the yellow frame railroad station hardly a block from his house. He had just come back from talking to the agent to find out the latest expected arrival time of the train from Anchorage. It would be in Nenana shortly before eleven o'clock, not many minutes from now. Shannon felt a twinge of nervousness, but he was pleased that Wetzler had selected him to make the first lap with the serum. Suddenly through the cold night air he heard the far-off, plaintive cry of a locomotive whistle. He kissed his wife good-by and started back to the station. His hurrying footsteps squeaked on the dry snow.

As the train slowed to a stop with a final hiss of steam, Shannon saw the conductor, carrying a package, step off and look searchingly up and down the platform. Knight smiled in recognition when he saw Shannon walking toward him in his fur trail clothes.

"Here's the serum," he said without preliminaries, handing Shannon the cylindrical package; and then he took a piece of paper from his pocket and gave that to the musher. "These are the directions the doctor in Anchorage gave me for its care on the trip," Knight added. As Shannon thanked him and started off, the conductor shouted after him, "Good luck!"

A few people came out in the cold for a few minutes to see "Wild Bill" off when he lashed the serum to his sled. After a quick wave he untied the snubline and stood momentarily on the brake. Then, to a shout, his nine malamutes surged forward and the great serum drive had begun.

As Shannon crossed to the east bank of the Tanana River and headed north his nine-dog team warmed to the run. With an easy lope the dogs followed the well-marked trail along the bank of the winding river. Occasionally the trail dipped down onto the frozen river for a short distance, but sharp ridges (where the ice had been thrown up by pressure from the current during fall freeze-up) made traveling on the bank faster. Directly behind him the few lights of Nenana faded into the night as the miles slipped by.

Shannon had been discharged from the Army a few years before. He had been stationed at Fort Gibbon at Tanana, where he was a blacksmith in the Quartermaster Corps. He shod the horses that were used for winter freighting of heavy equipment when the snow was not too deep. During his duty at Tanana, Shannon had become interested in sled dogs, and whenever he had the opportunity he had driven the Signal Corps teams used in maintaining the telegraph land lines.

Although slight of build, "Wild Bill" Shannon was well coordinated and strong. He had both a temper and a sense of humor. His nickname was derived from these combined characteristics. During his Army tour of duty he had come to love the solitude of the wilderness and determined to stay on in Alaska after his discharge. (Years later his passion for the wilderness would cost him his life: He was killed by a grizzly bear while prospecting alone.)

As the first light of dawn silhouetted 3,000-foot Murphy's Dome to the east, Shannon felt a sharper, telltale pinching of his nostrils as he breathed. He had come to a colder pocket of air and knew that the temperature was not far from 50° below zero. A ten to twenty-degree variation in temperature often occurred within a few miles along the river valleys. Shannon slowed his dogs to a trot so they would not frost their lungs. He was over halfway to Tolovana and calculated he could finish the fifty-two-mile trip by noon, even at the necessarily slower speed. As the team climbed a small hill Shannon ran behind the sled to warm up.

At 6 A.M. Wednesday, January 28, the telephone rang at Seppala's house at Little Creek, a few miles from Nome. Summers was on the phone and told Seppala to start at once for the Yukon. He instructed Seppala to go slowly at first, making short daily runs to save his dogs. He pointed out that if Seppala met the serum in the vicinity of Nulato for the return trip to Nome, he would have to travel over six hundred miles for the round trip—nearly twice the distance the musher from Nenana would have covered. Summers said the board had received word that the serum had reached Nenana and that a team had started with the serum shortly before midnight. The message from Nenana that Summers relayed to Seppala failed to say that the serum would be carried down the Yukon in relays.

Leonhard Seppala dressed quickly in his warmest trail clothes: a squirrel parka, sealskin pants, and reindeer mukluks. He was a small, wiry man, whose Alaskan background and early childhood in Skjervoy, a Norwegian fishing village above the Arctic Circle, pre-eminently fitted him for the task ahead. Like many another immigrant, Seppala had come to Alaska to find gold. Instead of wealth he had found satisfaction and some measure of fame working with the dogs of the North.

Bedlam broke out in the dog corral when the dogs spotted their master coming from the house in his trail clothes. Every dog in the kennel wanted to be included in Seppala's plans. The veteran musher expertly hitched twenty dogs to the sled standing outside the kennel. He did not hitch Togo to the towline, but let the twelve-year-old dog run free on what is known as a loose lead. As Togo came up to him he spoke softly to the little Siberian. It was plain to see that a deep bond existed between man and dog. His other leader, Scotty, was hitched at the head of the team and would follow Togo on the trail.

Seppala then called his assistant and gave him instructions. He told the man that during his absence the remaining thirteen dogs would be used for any freight hauling that was necessary. He looked speculatively at the dejected dogs remaining in the corral and then pointed at one dog and said, "You can use Fox as the leader of the freight team."

Fox, Balto, and the other rejected dogs settled down resignedly when Seppala left the kennel yard.

ARCTIC OCEAN

SIBERIA

Bering Strait

SEWARD
PENINSULA

ALASKA

ARCTIC CIRCLE

Nome
Pt. Safety
Solomon
Bluff
Golovin
Norton Bay
Shaktolik
Norton Sound
Old Woman
Nulato
Bishop Mtn.
Galena
Whiskey Creek
Kokrines
Nine Mile
Kallands
Tanana
Fish Lake
Manley Hot Springs
Tolovana
Yukon R.

Unalakleet
Kaltag
Ruby
Tanana R.
Nenana
Fairbanks

Yukon R.

CANADA

Bering Sea

Yukon R.

ALASKA RANGE

Susitna R.

Cantwell
Summit

Anchorage

Seward

Gulf of
Alaska

ALASKA PENINSULA

FROM ANCHORAGE TO NOME

++++++++ By Railroad
————— By Dog Sled

Scale of Miles

0   50   100   150   200

Word spread in Nome that Seppala was leaving
to intercept the serum at a village somewhere along
the Yukon. Friends and well-wishers lined Front
Street to shout encouraging words to the diminu-
tive musher as his dog team trotted through town
eastward. Some of the men knew the meaning of
the white miles that lay between Nome and Nulato
and the endurance that would be required.

Over six hundred trail miles from Seppala, Shannon's team swung due west for Tolovana. Sometimes the trail followed the westward, serpentine
course of the river; sometimes it cut across country.
Ahead where the trail approached the north bank
of the Tanana, Shannon could see scrub trees outlining an island in the middle of the frozen river.
He knew that a little over a mile beyond the island
he would reach Tolovana. He was very tired and
the dogs were now moving with their heads low
to the ground. He urged a last burst of speed from
the exhausted animals that carried them a few minutes later into the little settlement.

Another team was waiting outside the roadhouse,
and Dan Green, his friend, shouted a greeting.
Shannon told the other musher his trip had been
uneventful, but Green had bad news. He explained

to Shannon that the last message received from Nome indicated a rapid spread of the epidemic. Green told the tired driver that fifteen new cases and four deaths had been reported.

After reading the instructions, the two men took the serum into the roadhouse to warm it for fifteen minutes before Green started for Manley Hot Springs, thirty-one miles away.

V   ALONG THE YUKON

Spurred by the realization of the growing epidemic, Green drove his dogs to their utmost. The
trail to Manley Hot Springs headed due west for
ten miles, cutting across a six-mile-deep southward
bend in the Tanana. Five miles from Tolovana the
route passed between a small unnamed lake and
a low cluster of mountains to the north. The temperature had risen to $-30°$, but suddenly Green
was driving into a twenty-mile-per-hour wind
blowing down the slopes of the nearby hills. The
blast-freezing effect of the wind chilled the musher
to the bone.

Green stopped once to untangle his dogs after they had tried to break away in pursuit of a flock of ptarmigan, the snow-colored northern grouse. He removed his mittens to gain dexterity, and his fingers were slightly frosted by the time he was done a few minutes later. Now paralleling the river again, he had driven at last beyond the flow of air coming down the mountain slope. He sped past a trapper's cabin and knew his run would end in five miles.

At Manley Hot Springs, Johnny Folger's team was harnessed and tied outside the log roadhouse. Folger was roused from his chair close to the roaring wood-burning stove by the staccato barking of his dogs. He opened the door as Green drew up.

"Dan, go inside and warm up," he said to Green as he saw the driver painfully trying to untie the package of serum from his sled. Green nodded gratefully and brushed the ice from the wolverine ruff of his parka hood.

"Come inside when you get the serum off, and I'll give you the written directions," he told the third driver of the great race, adding that Folger could lash the package to the other sled after it had been warmed a short time.

Sam Joseph of the Tanana Indian tribe carried the diphtheria serum twenty-six miles, from Fish Lake to Tanana, at the remarkable speed of nine miles per hour. This picture shows Joseph today, standing outside his home in Tanana.

COURTESY OF SAM JOSEPH

In a few minutes Folger entered the inn. After warming the serum and exchanging a few hurried words about trail conditions with Green, Folger left the roadhouse and started his dogs toward Fish Lake. Darkness had fallen as the Indian driver headed his team through a pass between the low mountains north of Manley Hot Springs. Beyond the pass Folger could see the shadow of the trail stretching away until it disappeared in the distance on the starlit snow. He would make good time over his twenty-eight-mile lap of the serum relay race.

At Fish Lake in a little shelter cabin, thirty-five-year-old Sam Joseph and his team of seven mala-

mutes waited. Sounds carried far in the clear, cold
air. Long before he could see Folger, he could hear
his shouted commands to his dogs, and as they drew
closer he heard the padding of the dogs' feet on the
packed snow.

Joseph, also an Athabascan Indian, had finished
hitching his dogs to the sled when Folger arrived.
Again the serum was taken into the cabin for
warming. The mushers unwrapped the covering
and placed it close to the fire. Someone along the
trail had wrapped a piece of fur around the canvas
as additional protection against the cold. After the
allotted warming period, the serum was taken outside and tied to Joseph's sled. The broad-shouldered,
swarthy musher sped into the night, headed for
Tanana and home, a town at the junction of the
Tanana and Yukon rivers twenty-six miles away.

Sam Joseph was of the Tananas, a once-fierce interior tribe called "the people of the mountains,"
belonging to the general category of Yukon Indians. Although Joseph's forefathers were feared
by other tribes, once a year Tanana acted as host to
all the tribes of interior Alaska. A general amnesty
was declared and Indians for many miles came to
the village at the confluence of the two great rivers

for feasting, dancing, and competitive sports.

Until three years previously the Army had gar-
risoned Fort Gibbon at Tanana as maintenance
headquarters for the telegraph land line along the
Yukon, and to see that peace was kept in roistering
gold camps and among the interior Indian tribes.
The Army post was abandoned when its usefulness
was outlived.

At Tanana the temperature was recorded of-
ficially at 38° below zero on Thursday, January
29. Despite the cold, Joseph ran the twenty-six
miles to the Indian village, where his wife and children waited for him, in the remarkable time of two
hours and forty minutes, averaging better than
nine miles per hour. Joseph did not realize that his
arrival in Tanana, and his fast time, would be telegraphed outside and that thousands would read his
name. He was simply doing a job as well as he knew
how.

At Tanana still another Indian, Titus Nickoli,
waited his turn to carry the serum thirty-four miles
farther west.

Hour after hour, day and night, the antitoxin
was carried over the cold, white, monotonous miles
by stoically uncomplaining drivers and their

rugged, obedient dogs. These men accepted as natural the obligation to do what they could to help the people of Nome. They expected no pay for their efforts. In the North, then and still today, there is an unwritten code that demands help for anyone in distress. People are never too busy to assist one another—perhaps because they know that men must band together to survive in a country where at times the elements seem bitterly opposed to man's intrusion.

In the States certain newspapers and news agencies had begun to commercialize the event. They had come to realize that they could sell newspapers by carrying colorful stories of the dramatic race. With few facts available, reporters and editors let their imaginations run. The purple prose of "howling winds and minus 60° temperatures" along the route became the order of the day. Had they been able to report the event accurately, the bare facts would have been enough. How many of their readers could run thirty to fifty miles at subzero temperatures over a desolate frozen trail without stopping? How many of them would wade into a melee of snarling, snapping, part-wolf dogs to stop a fight and straighten tangled harness? What per-

centage of their readers would push off into a vast
white wilderness with the frightening knowledge
that a trail accident or a blizzard could mean slow
death by freezing? Certainly these uncompromis-
ing hazards belonged to the daily lives of the men
who carried the serum, but that did not make them
any less dangerous. (Four of the drivers who participated in the serum race later met wilderness deaths
by drowning or freezing.)

Thirty-four miles on from Tanana, at Kallands,
Nickoli passed the serum to Dave Corning. Corning kept up the relentless pace, driving past Gold
Mountain, named by an optimistic early prospector,
to the Nine Mile mail cabin (nine miles along the
mail run from Birches to Kokrines), averaging
eight miles per hour for twenty-four miles. At the
Nine Mile shelter house Edgar Kalland, the next
musher, warmed the serum before sprinting for
Kokrines.

Darkness had fallen again on the trail that lay
along the ice of the frozen Yukon. To the north
the dark mass of the Kokrine Hills rose abruptly
from the bank of the river and towered impassively
over Kalland and his running dogs. From time to
time the deep silence of the night was broken by

the grinding of the sled's ironbark runners on ridges of ice.

At the next relay point, thirty miles away, Harry Pitka, also part-Indian, watched his Indian wife make a new pair of dress moccasins in their cabin at Kokrines. The hide was moose that she had scraped and tanned to a golden brown over an alderwood fire in the autumn. Now she was sewing on a band of decorative white caribou around the tops before finishing them with beads and drawstrings tipped with pompoms. The moccasins were eight inches high and would be very warm unless they became wet. Unlike the sealskin of the Eskimo mukluks, the moosehide was porous and readily absorbed water.

Pitka had been a mail driver the previous year, but for some reason he had not been rehired by the mail contractor for the winter of 1924–25. He wondered whether he would be back on the mail run the following year—he needed the money, his family was growing.

When Kalland arrived, the transfer was made quickly to Pitka's waiting sled. The short, wiry musher owned a seven-dog team and made the next thirty miles to Ruby at better than nine miles per

The town of Ruby on the Yukon River was considerably busier in 1910, when this picture was taken, than when Harry Pitka and Bill McCarty stopped there during the 1925 serum race.

hour. Although it continued cold, the weather favored the speeding team. There was no powdery new snow to slow the packed trail, and the nights remained clear. It seemed for a while as though the elements were sympathetic, but this illusory friendliness was soon to be withdrawn; there were still four hundred miles of trail to Nome.

Bill McCarty, a dog musher and miner in the fading gold-strike town of Ruby, on the south bank of the Yukon, continued the exhausting drive toward the Bering Sea.

When the phone call had come over the Signal Corps' land line asking for a team to carry the serum, McCarty was the only experienced musher available in Ruby. He drove dogs for Alex Brown, and so he picked the seven best dogs from Brown's twenty-seven-dog kennel, with Prince as the leader.

Ruby had become famous for its annual dog team race, the Ruby Derby, and Brown, or the "Digo Kid," and his fleet team were well known.

McCarty's destination was Whiskey Creek, twenty-eight miles down the river. The stream had received its name in earlier days when unscrupulous whites had used it to cache contraband whiskey to sell to the Indians. It was now a main exchange point on the mail run and headquarters for the mail teams along this section of the river.

A few miles out of Ruby, McCarty encountered a brief but heavy snowstorm. During the hour it lasted, McCarty thought of the suffering in Nome and drove his dogs as hard as he could despite the handicap of poor visibility.

At the Creek, Edgar Nollner waited patiently. The mercury in the thermometer outside the cabin registered $-40°$. It was ten o'clock Thursday night and would probably get colder before morning. Twenty-one-year-old Nollner was counting on his eight-year-old lead dog, Dixie, to set a fast pace to Galena. A few years before, Dixie had led his team to victory in a six-mile race at Ruby, beating his nearest competitor by the wide margin of six minutes.

Finally McCarty and his panting dogs came in view around a bend in the trail. A few minutes later Ed Nollner was on his way to Galena, twenty-four miles away.

Nollner pushed his seven big gray malamutes as fast as they would go. His older brother George was waiting at Galena as the next relay driver. Ed was making sure no one could criticize his speed on the serum drive.

The two brothers spoke briefly as they transferred the precious cargo to George's sled. George had been married just a few days. He was reluctant to leave his bride and the warm cabin, but he knew the faster he drove the eighteen miles through the cold night to Bishop Mountain, the quicker he could return home to Galena.

Young Charlie Evans was standing by at Bishop Mountain with a team of nine dogs. The twenty-two-year-old half-breed was the son of the white village storekeeper and an Indian woman. He was a friend of both the Nollners.

From breakup in late May, until freeze-up in the fall, Evans acted as a Yukon River pilot, guiding the freight barges and paddle-wheelers around the ever-shifting sand bars of the continent's third largest river.

As Evans waited for Nollner the weather turned bitterly colder. The many-fingered white and pale green northern lights pulsing and flickering overhead were fading into gray dawn when at last he heard George Nollner in the distance. The young bridegroom was singing an Athabascan love song as he neared the end of his grueling journey.

The two friends took the serum into the cabin and warmed it for nearly an hour. They were afraid the piercing cold would freeze the liquid on the trail to Nulato unless it was well heated before the start.

At last Evans left the warmth of the cabin and headed for the Indian village of Nulato. It was five o'clock, Friday morning, fifty-four hours since the serum had started its journey at Nenana. The broad river stretched away before him through a silent and motionless world. He later said the temperature had fallen to 64° below zero when he forced himself and his dogs to start for the next village on the mail trail.

Ten miles along the sled trail from Bishop Mountain, where the east mouth of the Koyukuk River flows into the Yukon, Evans came to open water. The fast-running, suppressed waters of the converging rivers had eroded away the surface ice, and for half a mile Evans carefully skirted the dangerous overflow and the open river. Moisture in the warmer air rising from the water was instantly condensed and chilled into minute ice crystals. A two-foot-deep layer of dense ice fog lay along the trail. From time to time Evans drove into a tongue of the drifting fog and only the eerie sight of his dogs' heads and tails rising out of the white blanket told him that they were still on firm ice.

Five miles farther, the musher came to the village of Koyukuk. His father, visiting there, urged Evans to stop and warm up. The young driver was chilled through, and tempted; but he told his father he was afraid that if he stopped then, he might not be able to get his dogs started again. He was halfway to Nulato and pushed on. Evans had two borrowed dogs on his nine-dog team. A short distance from Koyukuk the two began to stiffen up and move painfully. Their groins were freezing. (The groin is the only place huskies are without heavy fur and vulnerable to extreme cold, especially if the dogs have been frozen before.) There was nothing Evans could do. He did not have rabbit-skin covers for them. (Both dogs later died.) As the sun climbed higher it gradually became warmer. Evans pulled into Nulato at 10 A.M. It had been a cruel thirty-mile run.

The little Indian village of Nulato, the home

of musher Tommy Patsy, had once been an important settlement. It was the site of the first Russian fort and trading post in interior Alaska. In 1851 the neighboring Koyukuks, the most feared interior Indians, attacked Nulato under cover of darkness, and after burning the fort, massacred the entire Russian garrison and most of the Indians there. Tommy Patsy knew the legend of his warring forefathers only through tales told by the village elders.

The copper-skinned Indian driver lashed the serum to his sled and with the best dogs in the village, dashed onto the river ice for the final leg of the race along the Yukon before the trail headed cross-country for the Bering Sea. Kaltag was thirty-six miles away, and he would make a supreme effort to get there in the shortest time possible. Trail conditions were ideal; the snow was packed and the light good. The mail trail from Nulato to Kaltag ran in a nearly straight line. Patsy made the distance in only three and a half hours, averaging slightly better than ten miles per hour. His was the fastest individual speed in the serum drive.

Back in Nulato, childlike, the Indians momentarly turned the grim serum race into a sport.

Evans won a betting pool by guessing closest the elapsed time of Patsy and his dogs.

From Kaltag the nature of the epic race would change gradually. The trail that for 390 miles had followed the Tanana and Yukon valleys now swung southwest into the hills and away from the river. For seventy-five miles it would follow the undulations of hill-born streams, climbing and then descending until it reached the Bering Sea at Unalakleet.

From there, north and west to Nome, the mercurial northern elements were waiting to test the last teams, both men and dogs, to their limit.

VI "FAIRBANKS IS STANDING BY..."

Even a crisis such as Nome was facing can produce a touch of comic relief. As the dog teams raced toward Nome, Fairbanks became more shrill and querulous in demanding that aircraft take over the delivery of the serum.

Hurried preparations were made to ready a plane for the flight. Glowing editorials appeared daily in the *Fairbanks News Miner* on the superiority of planes over dog teams.

"Wrong Font" Thompson, manager and editor of the newspaper, wrote: "Fairbanks could help Nome . . . if Washington could listen to Delegate Sutherland and realize the FRIENDLY NORTH has passed from the dog team stage into the airship class."

The editorial added optimistically: "Planes could be ahead of dog teams unless our ships went down and this would not happen."

Roy S. Darling, a former Navy pilot who was in Fairbanks on court business as special investigator for the Department of Justice, volunteered to fly Rodebaugh's plane if the Justice Department gave him permission. Ralph T. Mackie, Anchorage newspaperman and former member of the Royal Canadian Air Force, volunteered his services as mechanic to accompany Darling on the trip.

When dog teams were given the mission of carrying the antitoxin to Nome, Fairbanks refused to quit. The newspaper, and leading citizens with an interest in the Fairbanks Airplane Company, lobbied to have the plane intercept the serum at some point down the Yukon and to continue on to Nome with it.

There was no official refusal of this suggestion, but instead a silent wait-and-see attitude was taken on the part of the governor's office and other responsible agencies.

Troubles plagued the airplane enthusiasts. Ralph Mackie noted that temperatures along the route averaged −46° and sagely commented that it would be "impossible to equip men for a flight in the prevailing temperatures."

From somewhere word filtered into the Fairbanks newspaper office that James O'Brien, a movie cameraman and ex-member of the Royal Flying Corps, was in Ruby and would accompany Darling from there to Nome. The paper, with cheerful disregard for syntax, noted, "James O'Brien is waiting at Ruby with seven decorations" to go on to Nome.

While the flyers marked time for temperatures to moderate, mechanics assembling and testing the plane were beset with cold-weather mechanical difficulties. The engine oil would congeal into a molasseslike substance before the engine could be started. They would solve one problem only to be confronted with another.

Nevertheless, the *News Miner* continued its morale-boosting editorials. On Saturday, January 31, Thompson told his subscribers: "Fairbanks is standing by, lashed to the mast by Washington, beating its sourdough wings off trying to rush to the help of its friends and is restrained from so doing."

On this same day, the S.S. *Alameda* sailed from Seattle for Seward, Alaska, with 1,100,000 units of diphtheria antitoxin aboard, to back up the first shipment of 300,000 units being rushed westward by dog team. Perhaps a plane could carry the second shipment of serum from Fairbanks to Nome.

Finally, a wire-service news bulletin stated that the weather had warmed along the Yukon for the first time in two weeks; but with the warmer weather the flyers now faced "the peril of snowstorms." Another would-be flyer's name appeared fleetingly in newsprint. The story added that a Sergeant Farnsworth of the U.S. Army Air Service would accompany pilot Darling.

At least Darling was now free to go. Editor Thompson told the citizens of Fairbanks: "The Department of Justice and Navy Department wired permission to Roy Darling to fly his head off if he wishes to without expense to the Government."

It finally became apparent even to the most partisan flying boosters that the Rodebaugh plane would not be off the ground before the serum reached Nome by dog team. Nevertheless, with unquenchable enthusiasm, the airplane proponents went ahead with plans to carry the second batch of serum, due in Seward February 7, to Nome.

But these plans, too, went awry. On a final testing of the plane at Fairbanks' Weeks Field, the flyers finally bowed to defeat. Mr. Lynch, one of the plane's ground crew, firmly grasped the wooden propeller of the biplane, preparatory to swinging the prop to start the engine. At the cry of "CONTACT!" something went wrong. As Lynch briskly pulled the propeller through, there was a series of sharp explosions and Lynch hurtled high into the air. He had been bundled up warmly and his overcoat had caught in the propeller as the engine fired.

Friends who ran to him where he lay crumpled on the ground were relieved to find that he was shaken but unhurt. His overcoat had been torn nearly off, and Lynch was saddened to find that a favorite ten-dollar pipe in his pocket had been broken.

This event was the culmination of a series of mishaps and discouraged further efforts to fly serum to Nome. Even Mr. Thompson sadly admitted that under certain conditions dogs were superior to planes.

Fairbanks' agitation to have the serum flown to

Nome did not fail entirely. Delegate Sutherland promised he would work in the coming year to persuade the Government to open airmail routes and establish airfields across Alaska, so that if another emergency occurred no Alaskan town would be isolated and far from help as Nome was at present. Sutherland's efforts bore fruit. Within a few years the drone of airplane engines would crisscross the great land, and emergency medical aid would be only a few hours away for all Alaskans.

The coming of the bush airplane would change Alaska's way of life, but nothing could ever erase the essential role the dog team had played in opening America's northernmost frontier to settlement.

VII   DR. WELCH AND
NURSE SEVILLE

As the days passed in Nome, Dr. Welch and the dedicated nurses of the missionary hospital were fighting a grim battle on two fronts. The doctor's first definite diagnosis of Richard Stanley's illness, followed by the six-year-old boy's death from diphtheria, prefaced a rapid spread of the disease. Exposure had been widespread, and daily the doctor's doorbell or telephone rang with increasing frequency. The call for the tired, anxious doctor was monotonously the same: A frightened voice would report a member of the family with a sore throat and fever—the dreaded first symptoms of diphtheria.

The 75,000 units of five-year-old serum lasted only a few days. By January 30, the Board of Health had recorded five deaths, twenty-two diagnosed cases, and thirty suspected cases of diphtheria, as well as fifty persons who definitely had been exposed to infection.

Doctor and Lula Welch were heart-stricken when some of their dearest friends came down with the dangerous disease. The burden of responsibility for the entire population weighed heavily on the well-liked little doctor, but to the people of Nome his face showed only calmness and determination. He radiotelegraphed a worried sister, Mrs. L. A. Bettcher, in New Haven, Connecticut: "We are working night and day and are going to keep at it until we get the best of it."

Panic was a second danger in the growing epidemic. Dr. Welch and the nurses knew the results of uncontrolled fear could be catastrophic. If, in order to escape the disease, frightened residents and their families started to slip away from Nome at night by dog team to other villages, the epidemic would undoubtedly engulf all of northwestern Alaska.

In an effort to check the spread of the disease and to allay fear, the Board of Health composed a quarantine message with instructions from Dr. Welch. The notice was carried on the front page of the *Nome Nugget* on January 24 and said in part:

An epidemic of diphtheria has broken out in Nome and if proper precautions are taken there is no cause for alarm. On the other hand, if parents do not keep their children isolated from other children, the epidemic may spread to serious proportions.

The message urged every parent to consider himself a quarantine officer and to prevent his child from coming in contact with others.

All children should be compelled to wash their faces and hands frequently during the day with some mild soap such as Ivory Soap. A strong soap is worse than none at all as it has a tendency to cause the face and hands to chap and crack and render them easily susceptible to the diphtheria germ.

The notice ended on a somber note:

Residents of outlying districts should refrain from coming to Nome until this epidemic has subsided, and every effort will be made on the part of officials to prevent the carriers of the disease from leaving Nome and thereby contaminating the adjacent camps.

Dr. Welch feared, however, that the disease was already smoldering in other communities. He suspected that an unidentified traveler had brought the germ to Nome. It was almost too much to hope that someone from Nome had not already infected outlying villages during the incubation period of the first cases.

It was for this reason that Dr. Welch refused Washington's offer to send seven doctors and sixteen nurses scattered throughout Alaska to Nome as soon as possible to assist him. To the offer, Dr. Welch wirelessed back: "Nurses are not needed here. We have four in the hospital and five who may be called in an emergency."

The doctor told the U.S. Public Health Department officials he was certain of his diagnosis and he felt the disease would strike other Alaskan communities. He added that in Nome both the natives and whites were cooperating in measures to combat the disease and that with the arrival of the serum and with increasing sunlight of the lengthening days, he hoped to have the situation well in hand.

Nevertheless, Dr. John Ventor, at Nulato on the Yukon, stood by to mush to Nome to assist the lone, courageous doctor should he ask for help.

As Dr. Welch plodded wearily on his rounds to

Dr. Curtis Welch had been interested in prospecting when he first came to Nome in 1906, but soon medicine was to occupy all of his time. He was the only doctor who remained in Nome when the gold rush ended, around 1910. "He's a rugged individualist . . . and this country suits him," said Mrs. Welch. This photograph was taken one year after the diphtheria epidemic, in 1926, while the doctor was taking a well-earned vacation.

UNDERWOOD & UNDERWOOD

care for the sick he thought back over his early medical training and nearly twenty years of practice in Alaska.

The appeal of gold and adventure that had drawn thousands to the Seward Peninsula in the early 1900s had also beckoned the young doctor to the Far North. In 1906 Dr. Welch turned his back on a promising medical career in Los Angeles and, accompanied by his plucky wife, headed for the raw and lusty gold camps of northern Alaska.

In the ensuing years he had never regretted his decision and from the beginning had felt a love and affinity for the great, silent—although at times tumultuous—land.

Dr. Welch's friends often had asked him why he

had not returned to further his career in a large American city. Certainly his background and training pointed to success, if not eminence, in his profession. But except for his brief World War I service in the Army Medical Corps, when he returned East and was directly commissioned a major just before the armistice, the doctor had remained in Alaska, going to the States only every eight or ten years for a well-earned vacation.

Curtis Welch had been graduated from Yale's College of Medicine in 1897. From there, his training was rounded out while interning at the large Los Angeles General Hospital. It was during his internship that he found himself falling in love with a nurse, a pretty Southern girl who had been an actress before turning to nursing. They soon became engaged.

After completing his internship and residence, Dr. Welch received an enviable plum. He was offered, and accepted, a job as assistant to one of Los Angeles' top surgeons, Dr. E. A. Bryant. On the strength of this good news and promised security, he and Lula were married.

In Nome, Dr. Welch placed a thermometer under Billy Lee's tongue and put cool fingers on his pulse. As he looked at the flushed and feverish face of the little boy he offered silent thanks that his training had been the best that could be obtained. It was not a substitute for antitoxin, but it helped him carry on until the serum arrived. During the doctor's practice in Los Angeles, he had found time for courses at the Harvard Medical Summer School as well as graduate work at Johns Hopkins and the New York Lying-in Hospital. Yes, he had come to Alaska well prepared, but even after many years he sometimes found the necessity of working alone and without a laboratory or the latest medical aids terribly hard.

Perhaps a key to his love for Alaska and reluctance to return to the States was revealed by something he said to a friend on his return from a vacation trip "outside." In comparing easy-going Alaskan social customs with those of his early home in New Haven, Connecticut, he said half seriously, "It gets on my nerves to have to be introduced to a man before I can speak to him."

Another key to the doctor's character as a man was revealed by the observation of an old Alaskan friend, Malcolm Smith, explorer and prospector. Smith told members of the Explorers' Club in New

York during the Nome epidemic: "During the gold days there were a number of doctors in Nome. But when the surface gold had vanished and the gold seekers deserted the former boom town, the doctors drifted out of the northland.

"But there was one doctor . . . who did not desert the ship. He was the small, dependable, but always modest Dr. Welch."

Smith reflectively added, "Dr. Welch, though he has grown gray-haired serving his fellow beings, has not accumulated much of the gold which once he walked over. He doctors all who come to him. If they have money, they pay; if they haven't, they don't. And a lot of them haven't it, which explains in part the doctor's lack of opulence."

When Lula Welch was asked about her good-natured husband, she smilingly replied, "He's a rugged individualist with a keen sense of humor, and this country suits him."

Dr. Welch tried prospecting for a while when he first came to Alaska, but soon realized the people in Council, Candle, and other isolated gold-mining camps needed a doctor worse than he needed gold.

During the epidemic Nurse Emily Morgan, who had served overseas with the American Expeditionary Forces in World War I, helped lighten Dr. Welch's heavy burden. She assumed care of the patients in the hospital. As a quarantine measure no diphtheria cases were taken there, but Miss Morgan, with many years of medical experience, was able to relieve the doctor of much of his routine work in the missionary hospital so that he could concentrate his energies on combatting the epidemic. Throughout the trying period people were heartened and reassured to see her calm, smiling face as she went about her duties or on errands in the village.

Day and night Bertha Seville accompanied the doctor on his rounds to the sick. Nurse Seville was known and liked by everyone. The Eskimos smiled shyly and affectionately at the plain but sympathetic woman who knew their customs and understood their ways.

Many of the natives and whites in Nome had an unreasoning fear of inoculation. Bertha Seville's patience and persistence helped the doctor overcome their resistance to treatment as they used the old serum on hand, and later the new serum when it arrived.

Mrs. Curtis Welch further increased the doctor's capabilities. A registered nurse, she took over the doctor's office duties. The Welches had no children, so through the years of her husband's medical practice she had been able to assist him. Now she performed all minor surgery for the doctor, handled the medical records, and acted as a buffer for him in dealing with the Board of Health and the U.S. Public Health Service so that his time could be entirely devoted to the emergency. In addition to these duties, Lula Welch found time to cook three meals a day for her tired husband. At night she would often sit with a sick child.

Others courageously volunteered their services, delivering food to the homes of the quarantined, realizing they were daily exposing themselves to the danger of infection.

As the dog teams carrying the serum sped westward, name after name was added to the list of the sick. Still, it was nearly miraculous that the list had not grown faster. Credit was due Dr. Welch and his nurses and the people of Nome, who cooperated and obeyed his instructions.

The hard-working doctor's delaying action was small consolation, however, to those who had been stricken. Diphtheria victims Minnie Englestadt, Billy Lee, James Gabriel, Ruth Cameron, Wallace

Anneletoolook, and many others tossed feverishly in their beds, their throats burning with pain. To them the anxiously awaited antitoxin meant release from suffering and hope of recovery.

For a few it was already too late. In the Barnett, Stanley, and Rothacker homes there was a heartbreaking void and the fervent wish that other Nome families be spared the loss of a loved child.

As conditions in Nome became more critical, the chairman of the Board of Health called a hurried meeting with the other board members. These men discussed the urgency of the situation with Dr. Welch. It was apparent to them all that each day that passed without antitoxin was a victory for diphtheria. They concurred quickly that additional dog teams should be spaced at intervals along the trail from Unalakleet to Nome. In this way Seppala's run would be shortened. Summers said, "If we set up additional relays along Norton Sound, the utmost speed can be maintained without having the serum stop en route for one minute."

Two well-known mushers in Nome were called and instructed to start east to intercept the serum. Gunnar Kaasen was to wait at Bluff, some fifty miles away, and later Ed Rohn was stationed at Pt.

Safety, for the last twenty-one-mile sprint of the journey to Nome.

Kaasen was to deliver the board's message to Charlie Olson, part owner of a quartz mine and the roadhouse proprietor at Bluff, to head east with his dogs and meet Seppala when the little Norwegian reached Golovin, seventy-eight miles from Nome.

When Olson left Kaasen at Bluff after receiving the board's request on Saturday, January 31, it was 24° below zero, with overcast skies and a rising wind. He wondered if the weather would further deteriorate into a full blizzard.

As an additional measure, Summers sent a wireless message to Charles Traeger, storekeeper in Unalakleet, to "spare no expense" in arranging for teams to carry the serum north until they could transfer the serum package to Seppala's sled. Everything possible had now been done. Nome waited.

VIII ON TO THE BERING SEA

Over the huge expanse of western Alaska the dog teams carrying the serum inched ever closer to the Bering Sea.

Jackscrew, a small, muscular Indian known along the Yukon for his unusual strength, urged greater speed from his struggling dogs as they climbed higher into the sloping valleys of the low mountains between Kaltag and Unalakleet. Darkness had fallen and it had begun to snow lightly before he reached a mail cabin, twenty-two miles from his destination at the Old Woman shelterhouse. Jackscrew passed the cabin without stopping.

On and on he jogged tirelessly, and to lighten the sled he did not ride the runners until he had traversed the Kaltag Divide and felt the dogs gather speed on the downward trail leading to Norton Sound. It was 9:10 P.M. Friday when ahead on the trail an oil lantern on a pole over the door of the Old Woman cabin shone softly through the black night, marking the end of Jackscrew's run. The tough little Indian and his dogs had averaged almost six miles per hour for forty miles over uneven, difficult terrain to bring the serum a step closer to Nome.

Fifteen minutes after Jackscrew arrived, Victor Anagick, a full-blooded Eskimo, took the serum and headed for Unalakleet, his home, thirty-four miles away. Anagick was a clerk for Unalakleet storekeeper Charles Traeger and was driving the storekeeper's eleven-dog team. Traeger had sent Anagick to Old Woman when the message from Nome arrived asking for additional relays. Anagick reached Unalakleet six hours later, at 3:30 Saturday morning.

In Nome, 207 trail miles away, the temperature registered 19° below zero and was falling. East and south along Norton Sound to Unalakleet the stars were blotted out by lowering clouds, and the increasing wind blew gustily from the northeast.

From Unalakleet to Nome the weather and the serum drive would undergo dramatic changes. No longer would the trail follow the sheltering valleys of the great interior rivers, but would skirt the exposed shoreline of the frozen Bering Sea, and, at the discretion of the drivers, at times would cut across the frozen bays of Norton Sound to save valuable hours and shorten the distance.

The Bering Sea, though frozen, could be capricious and treacherous. Open channels would unexpectedly appear, and with a strong offshore wind the ice would sometimes break up and move out to sea. Through the years many a luckless seal-hunting Eskimo and an occasional musher had been lost on the unpredictable sea ice.

Far out on the Bering Sea the wind whipped the open water into squall-marked, white-ridged waves, and the fast ice bordering the shore creaked and groaned ominously to the rhythm of the ground swell rolling in under the surface.

Myles Gonangnan listened carefully as Traeger's assistant, Edward Bradley, gave him instructions on carrying the serum north. Bradley faced the rising wind and then looked out over the bleak whiteness of Norton Sound. Finally he said to Gonangnan, "We can't risk the ice. You must go along the hills skirting the shore. It will be slower, but safer."

Gonangnan, a full-blooded Eskimo, had lived in Unalakleet for all of his twenty-eight years. He had married a handsome Eskimo girl, a tribal princess from a village further north. They had two girls and a boy. Myles's life was full. He hunted, fished, and trapped. With his dog team he sometimes freighted goods from St. Michael to Unalakleet for storekeeper Charles Traeger.

After Bradley had finished reading the instructions accompanying the serum, he told Gonangnan to stop at Eban, an Eskimo settlement twenty-five miles away, and warm the serum for fifteen minutes before driving on to Shaktolik, a total distance of forty miles.

Myles knew it would be slow going, as there had been six inches of new snow in the past few days and he would have to break trail all the way. (Often the mail contractors found it necessary to hire a man to snowshoe ahead of the dogs after a heavy snowfall to pack the trail, particularly if the mail load was heavy.) Gonangnan forced his eight dogs to go as fast as they could through the soft, virgin powder. They were strong mixed-breeds but not very fast. Between four and five miles per hour was the best speed Gonangnan could average, but his team kept that pace steadily as they broke trail along the foothills bordering the sound.

The Eskimo was proud of his team's stamina and weight-pulling capability rather than their speed. He had once carried a load of freight to St. Michael, sixty miles distant, and after resting one hour there had mushed back to Unalakleet, making the round trip of 120 miles within a twenty-four hour period.

At Eban he warmed the serum as he had been instructed and then ploughed on. It was only fifteen miles farther to Shaktolik, but it was now blowing so hard that eddies of drifting, swirling snow passing between the dogs' legs and under their bellies made them appear to be fording a fast-running river. The sea horizon and outline of the treeless hills blended into the overcast and were soon lost in the growing storm. To Gonangnan it seemed that he had become the stationary center of a gray-

Gunnar Kaasen (at left) and two other men posed for this picture to show the way in which the serum package was transferred during the race itself. The drivers hoped that the bulky wrapping would protect the antitoxin from the bitterly cold temperatures, but it froze in spite of their precautions.

white world without sky or earth or distances.

Ahead at Shaktolik, Henry Ivanoff, a part-Russian Eskimo, waited for Gonangnan.

As soon as Gonangnan arrived at Shaktolik the serum was transferred to Ivanoff's waiting sled and Ivanoff started north. Hardly a half mile from town Ivanoff ran into trouble. His dogs picked up the scent of reindeer on the trail and tried to break away to follow the herd.

Ivanoff drove the steel two-spike sled brake into the snow to halt the half-crazed team. As the sled slowed to a stop, two of the frustrated dogs turned on each other, and in seconds the other dogs joined the snarling, yelping fray. As the musher waded into the tangle of harness and snapping malamutes, swinging the butt of his whip to restore order, he saw a dog team coming toward him from the north.

As the team neared, Ivanoff recognized Seppala's famous Siberians (the only huskies of this type in the serum drive) and the little man riding the runners at the rear of the sled. He waved and yelled at Seppala, but the gale swept his shouted words away. Seppala did not hear him and only waved back as he turned his team to the right to pass Ivanoff. The Eskimo shouted again as he swung past, and this time Seppala heard faintly the words, "Serum—*turn back!*"

At first the Nome musher thought he had misunderstood the stranger. He still had 140 miles to go to reach Nulato, where he expected to meet the team coming down the river. He had been beyond telephone communication with Nome for three days and did not know of the decision to shorten the relays for greater speed. When he looked over his shoulder he saw the other musher waving him back. No, he had not been mistaken; the man had said "serum."

Seppala's dogs had put on a burst of speed when they had first scented the other team. Now with Shaktolik in sight (which meant food and rest) the team did not want to stop. Seppala's shouted "Gee" to Togo and Scotty had little effect until they came to a stretch of packed snow where he was able to brake the sled and turn the disappointed dogs. When they returned to the Eskimo's team, Ivanoff placed the serum in Seppala's sled and handed the little Norwegian the written instructions.

Seppala had left Isaac's Point on the north side of Norton Bay, an arm of Norton Sound, that morning and had mushed forty-three hard miles across the ice to Shaktolik. Although the rising wind had made the trip thoroughly uncomfortable, the wind had been at his back, helping him and his dogs toward their destination. Now with the temperature thirty degrees below zero, he would have to face into the merciless gale and in the darkness retrace his route across the uncertain ice.

IX   TOGO

Both men knew that although Ivanoff's dogs were fresh, Seppala's championship team and the veteran musher would, in all probability, make better time through the gathering storm, where Seppala would draw on his recognized skill and vast experience.

Out on the trail "The Hardy Norseman" often made one hundred miles in a day's run if the weather was favorable. During the year of 1916 he had covered a total of seven thousand miles by dog team.

Now, with the wind whipping the stinging snow

into the tunnel made by his parka hood, Seppala shouted to his little lead dog, Togo, to start the team back.

He later said, "There was nothing for it but to face the music. The dogs did their best, and I drove as if we were in a race."

Togo yipped back at his teammates and trotted northward as the signal to start. The string of double-harnessed Siberians surged forward, and as the towline became taut the sled leaped ahead.

Seppala and a few other mushers had proven conclusively that the Siberian was a superior sled dog in speed and stamina. They had become important as Alaskan racing and work dogs after 1909, when Fox Maule Ramsay, a young Scottish nobleman with mining interests in Nome, imported a large number from the Kolima River area in Siberia. From that time on, Ramsay's Siberians and their many descendants won more than their share of famous Alaskan dog races. Seppala found the Siberian huskies possessed machinelike endurance at a steady fast pace. Because of their relatively small size (fifty to sixty pounds, and twenty-one to twenty-three inches height) they were not favored by most mushers for heavy freighting.

Foxlike in appearance, gray-white in color, Siberians have pointed noses, prick ears, and bushy tails curling up over their backs. They are gentle, making good pets for children—unlike some malamutes with their vicious wolf strain—and require little food. Because of their small size Seppala's famous team was referred to jokingly as "those little plume-tailed rats."

Togo embodied the best qualities of the breed, although as a puppy his future had not seemed promising. He had been bred and raised in the mining company kennels, managed by Seppala, but belonged to a man named Anderson. Small, even for a Siberian, Togo as a pup was mischievous and hard to handle. When Togo was about six months old, Anderson became disgusted with him and gave the dog to Seppala. Seppala, in turn, gave the pup to a friend, a woman who wanted a dog for a pet.

The sheltered life did not appeal to the young dog, and the more he was pampered and fed choice tidbits, the worse his conduct became. On several occasions he even snapped at his new mistress, showing all the signs of becoming a full-fledged canine delinquent. Togo repeatedly escaped from his new home and ran back to his birthplace and the kennels at Little Creek. It was finally agreed that Seppala take him back.

As he grew older Togo delighted in following his master and the team out on a run, but made himself a nuisance by occasionally nipping one of the harnessed dogs' ears and then running away to avoid retaliation.

When Togo was eight months old, Seppala had to make a lengthy trip to Dime Creek, a mining camp up the Koyuk River. In order to keep the little husky from following the team, Seppala locked him in the dog corral, a small yard enclosed with a seven-foot-high wire mesh fence. As an added precaution he told his assistant not to let Togo out for a day or two.

That night, after Seppala had left and everyone was asleep, Togo decided to escape. In the attempt, he almost cleared the seven-foot fence, but one of his hind legs caught in a mesh of the wire near the top. His puppy squeals brought the kennel boss on the run to the enclosure. He found Togo hanging down on the outside of the corral. When the man cut him down, the little dog rolled nimbly over and fled into the night.

On his way to Dime Creek, Seppala spent the

Leonhard Seppala and his wife are seen here with Togo. The famous racing dog was small, even for a Siberian husky, and as a pup he had shown little promise. But after the young Togo practically forced his master to test him as a sled dog, Seppala realized that he had found what he had sought for years—a "born leader."

first night at Solomon, thirty-three miles from Nome. In the morning, before daybreak, he started his team toward Bluff. He had gone only a few miles when through the murk of dawn he saw a small animal running in front of the team. At first he thought it was a fox, but soon discovered his error. The animal ran up and nipped the leader on the ear. It was Togo.

There was nothing for Seppala to do but take the young dog with him. That day Togo, running loose, created havoc by leading the team on a chase after a reindeer over a crusted section of the trail where the musher could not stop the runaway dogs. That was enough for Seppala. When the reindeer was out of sight and the dogs manageable again, he got an extra harness from the sled and hitched Togo in the wheel position (nearest the sled, a customary place for a new dog) where he could watch him.

Seppala was amazed at the transformation that took place. The eight-month-old pup immediately became all business and pulled harder than his grown teammates. The veteran musher kept moving the young dog farther ahead in the team every few miles, and before the end of the day Togo had been promoted to sharing the lead. Seppala realized he had found, by accident, something he had been trying to breed for years: a born leader. His judgment was correct; Togo, in a few years, became the most famous leader of his time.

X THE TREACHEROUS ICE

Now Togo was beginning his last great race. The small, wiry man and his team of dogs drove unflinchingly into the bitter-cold gale. They were not battling to win a coveted cup or cash prize; this time the stakes were higher—life or death for themselves and the people in Nome. Togo could not comprehend such complexities as a diphtheria epidemic, but he recognized and clearly understood the urgency in his master's voice. His pride of leadership and unquestioning obedience to Seppala would keep him going until he dropped of exhaustion, if necessary.

The old Siberian leader and his teammates were in top physical condition for the heartbreaking test of endurance that lay ahead. It had been four days since they had left Nome. Seppala had driven them at an easy pace to harden them for the long journey and to conserve their energy for the race homeward with the serum. The first day out they had traveled thirty miles, and thereafter had averaged fifty miles a day until reaching Shaktolik. Nevertheless, the driver and his dogs would need every ounce of their tremendous stamina and courage to reach Golovin, ninety-one miles away.

As Seppala and his team threaded their way northward to Ungalik over the snow-covered tundra and frozen marsh land of the inner shoulders of Cape Denbigh and Point Dexter jutting into the Bering Sea, he was faced with a hard decision. In a few miles he would come to the shore line of Norton Bay, where the shortest route to Nome lay in a northwest course, straight across twenty miles of open windswept ice to Isaac's Point. The wind had reached gale velocity and the driving snow was blinding. Seppala fully realized the awful danger inherent in the northeast gale. The ice of the bay could break up at any moment and be blown out to sea. In this dark, wind-filled world, he might not see or hear the open channels forming from the crumbling ice in time to avoid being trapped. He was familiar with the horrifying prospects of that possibility: drowning, freezing, or if he were very fortunate, being stranded on floating ice that later might be swept against shore ice, where he and the dogs could make their way to land.

His only alternative was to drive many miles farther inland along the coast of Norton Bay and cross where the bay narrowed and where the sheltered ice would be firmer and safer. But this route would add hours to his journey to Isaac's Point.

Seppala's little girl, Seigrid, had earlier contracted diphtheria and recovered. While he balanced the alternatives and measured his chances, Seppala thought of some of his good friends and their children who had been stricken and who were waiting for the antitoxin. The small, blue-eyed man made up his mind. He would take the short route to Isaac's Point and trust in God and the speed of his dogs to get him across before the ice went out.

There were few, if any, men in Alaska in 1925

better fitted physically and psychologically to take the calculated risk Seppala had decided upon. At forty-eight he was still in his prime. From the time of his boyhood in Norway, Seppala had led an athletic, outdoor life. As a young man he had gained a reputation as an excellent wrestler, and later, after coming to Nome, he had won all of the local skiing competitions before he had become interested in sled-dog racing. His lifelong physical training and conditioning would help him through the hard miles ahead.

The full force of the wind staggered the musher as Togo and Scotty led the team down the slope of the beach and out onto the ice of the bay. Seppala knew he would have to draw on all his reserves to make it to the north side of the sound. He would be forced to rely unquestioningly on Togo and his uncanny sense of direction to lead him to safety across the dark, treacherous miles of sea ice. For once he was thankful for one of Togo's faults.

The short-coupled little leader seemed to know instinctively that a straight line is the shortest distance between two points. Across the trackless tundra or the Bering Sea ice, Togo's unerring instinct for direction was a great asset; Seppala could go to sleep in the sled and his leader would take him to his destination. But when the trail followed a winding stream bed or skirted hills or other topographical obstacles, the asset became a liability. Togo would try to eliminate the turns, even if it meant climbing an almost vertical bank. It took all of Seppala's patience and skill to keep the little husky on the trail. He laughingly excused Togo's shortcoming to friends by saying that it was merely the eccentricity of genius.

An hour passed slowly, and although the team was making good time, Seppala knew that he had not reached the halfway point across the frozen bay. As he leaned into the furious wind he tried to listen for the telltale cracking and grinding that would preface a breakup. Either the wind was smothering any warning sounds or his luck was holding. He could not be sure which.

Occasionally Seppala passed over stretches of glare ice where the wind had scrubbed the snow from the glassy surface. The dogs slipped and sometimes fell, and once the light hickory racing sled was blown sideways, pulling the struggling dogs with it. In other places the ice had become rough and uneven, but he was thankful there were no ice spears to lame the dogs. Sometimes after a strong wind, pressure caused the ice to form needle-sharp spears. Mushers then had to put flannel boots on the dogs' feet to keep them from being cut by the sharp ice.

Seppala's team's remarkable speed, as well as the speed of many of the teams behind and ahead of him on the trail, was the result of a gradual evolution in Alaskan sled-dog breeding and selection. During the period of the gold strikes and for a few years after the turn of the century, huskies were judged primarily for their size and strength. The lone prospector had to freight hundreds of pounds of gear and food to his distant claim to survive the long, cold winters. The Indian trapper was interested only in the load-carrying capacity and stamina of his malamutes to bring in his firewood or to take his furs many miles to a trading post.

In the beginning even the mail teams ran to heft rather than speed. The mail loads were supposed to be limited to eight hundred pounds, but at times ran as high as fifteen hundred pounds. Then it was necessary to add extra dogs to make up a team of seventeen to twenty-five dogs, sometimes towing two or more sleds lashed together.

After the excitement of the gold rush subsided, residents of Nome and other small Alaskan communities looked around for some way to pass the dark winter months. All mining ceased after the first heavy snowfall, and except for essential services, most Nomeites tended to hibernate during the winter. Card playing, reading, and talk around the roaring stove were the principal means of alleviating "cabin fever" or boredom.

After years of using dogs for freighting and transportation, it was a natural development that dog-team racing suddenly should become the Far North's major sport. In 1908 the Nome Kennel Club was founded, and under its gold and green colors the first major dog race in Alaska was organized and run. The All-Alaskan Sweepstakes was intended as an annual race for the best teams and drivers who could qualify for a grueling 408-mile course from Nome north across the Seward Peninsula to Candle and return.

Designed to test the stamina as well as the speed of the dogs and drivers, the trail crossed some of the bleakest and most desolate terrain in Alaska—including Death Valley, feared for its sudden arctic blizzards. The event, undoubtedly one of the great-

est tests of endurance in the annals of sport, captured the imagination of sporting enthusiasts not
only in Alaska but throughout the nation.

Each year after 1908, Nome hummed in prepa-
ration for the big race. The sweepstakes was held in
early spring, and throughout the preceding winter,
dog breeding and training was followed with the
intensity Bluegrass Kentuckians reserve for their
thoroughbreds. In Nome alone, aggregate betting
reached as high as a half-million dollars on a single
race. The purses for the winner ran to thousands of
dollars.

In 1910 "Iron Man" John Johnson made the
408-mile run in the incredible record time of sev-
enty-four hours and fifteen minutes. Scotty Allen,
perhaps the greatest musher of them all, won the
marathon race three times and figured in the money
for each of the eight races he entered. Allen's dogs
were a mixture of bird dog and malamute. Seppala
won the All-Alaskan Sweepstakes in 1915, 1916,
and 1917 with his Siberians. The annual race was
discontinued because of World War I and was
never revived.

However, beginning with the period of the
sweepstakes, fevered interest in racing spread

throughout Alaska. Even primitive Indians understood the rudiments of selective breeding, and everywhere dog owners tried to improve their strains for greater speed. No longer were size and strength the sole criteria of a good sled dog. Dog team racing became a popular pastime at native settlements along the Yukon, and the fifty-eight-mile Ruby Derby brought participating teams for hundreds of miles to the mining settlement on the south bank of the river. In 1916 Seppala set an unbroken record at Ruby of five hours and twenty-six minutes for the hilly, difficult fifty-eight-mile course.

In 1915, during World War I, the reputation of Nome's dogs had spread even to hard-pressed France. The French Government sent Army Lieutenant René Haas nine thousand miles to Nome to purchase dogs for supply use in the Vosges Mountains. Scotty Allen selected a large number of the northern sled dogs for the French lieutenant, and they later performed valiant combat service with the French Alpine Corps in country so rugged horses and mules could not be used for transporting food and ammunition.

Arctic explorers Captain Roald Amundsen and

Vilhjalmur Stefansson also turned to Nome for sled dogs for their famous expeditions. Togo was the son of a dog selected to make an over-the-icecap trip to the North Pole with Amundsen in 1910. Amundsen planned to enter the Arctic Ocean through the Bering Strait with his ship *Fram* and then float with the current-driven pack ice as close as possible to the Pole. The explorer then intended using dog teams for the final dash over the ice, hoping to be the first man to reach the North Pole.

When Admiral Peary discovered the Pole in 1909, the Amundsen expedition was abandoned and the dogs were turned over to Seppala.

This, then, was the background and heritage of the dogs and men in the serum race who were covering the distance from Nenana to Nome in less than a third of the estimated time, against odds of extreme cold and a furious, unrelenting blizzard.

Shortly before eight o'clock Saturday night Seppala thankfully stumbled up the bank of the north shore of Norton Bay. Minutes later through the darkness he could see the outline of an Eskimo sod igloo. He had spent the previous night there, although it seemed like days before to the weary man. Togo and his teammates, while battling through the storm, averaged an extraordinary seven-plus miles per hour for the return trip across the ice. They had traveled eighty-four miles that day without stopping to rest.

The musher put his tired team in the Eskimo's kennel and fed the ravening dogs a large ration of salmon and seal blubber before going into the igloo to warm himself and rest.

Seppala pulled the sled inside and read the instructions accompanying the serum. He then asked the Eskimo to build up the fire and undid the fur and canvas coverings of the serum package. The musher felt certain the serum had frozen but saw nothing in the instructions about breaking the seals on the paper cartons enclosing the vials. He placed the antitoxin as close to the fire as he dared and stretched out, hoping the blizzard would moderate while he rested. For the first time in more than five hundred miles, except for brief warming periods, the serum was temporarily halted on its journey to Nome.

Early on Sunday Seppala hitched the dogs to the sled. He estimated the temperature at below $-30°$. The blizzard was still raging and the wind, if anything, had increased, but he felt he could not wait longer to start for Golovin. The trail from Isaac's Point paralleled the shore line some distance out on the ice, cutting straight across the small bays and inlets.

An old Eskimo watched Seppala tie the serum to the sled, and after mentioning the high wind, hesitantly cautioned the famous driver, "Maybe ice not much good. Maybe breaking off and go out. Old trail plenty no good. Maybe you go more closer to shore."

Seppala shouted above the wind to thank the old man as he commanded his team to start. A short distance along the ice, he was grateful he had taken the Eskimo's suggestion, for even hugging the beach he came within a few feet of open water. The trail over which he had traveled the day before had broken off and had been carried out to sea.

At Creek River the elements seemed to go mad. The wind became so violent that Seppala wondered whether he would make it through to Golovin. The musher did not know the force of the wind, but he did know that winter gales of over sixty miles per hour occasionally occurred along the Bering Sea coast. The dogs began to stiffen up, and he stopped to rub them. After massaging the dogs, Seppala brushed the masklike shell of ice and snow from their faces and went on. He struggled past the Elim Mission and Walla Walla, along the coast, and then headed across Cape Darby, with eighteen miles left to Golovin.

Mile after slow mile he mushed on. He thought fleetingly of his old leaders: of Suggen, and also Kvick, with his wonderful trail sense. Then he looked ahead and saw the dim outline of his little leader loping steadily forward through the storm-filled world. No, those fine old dogs were not the equal of Togo; he had been the finest trail leader the musher had ever known. There would never be another dog to replace the little Siberian in Seppala's affection.

At last they reached Golovin, where Charlie Olson was waiting to take the serum. Seppala and his team had covered a grueling ninety-one miles. Olson watched the courageous dogs drop in their tracks from exhaustion as the Nome musher pulled up in front of Dexter's Roadhouse. The antitoxin was now seventy-eight miles from Nome.

XI   THE RAGING STORM

Forty-six-year-old bachelor Charles V. Olson
was an outstanding example of a disappearing breed
of Alaskan. A true sourdough, Charlie Olson embodied qualities that made the pioneer of the North
a unique human being. His hardihood, generosity,
and humor were unfailing; his kind of rough
strength and selfless courage are seldom encountered today. Olson had lived his entire adult life in
a country and during a period of time that required
physical and mental toughness to survive. The
northern frontier demanded a rigid code of conduct, and those who were too soft physically or too

selfish to conform to the unwritten laws fled Alaska.

An Alaskan pioneer shared his shelter or provisions with anyone in need—even if it meant he would have to tighten his own belt. A man's word was his bond and debts were scrupulously honored. A stranger's injury or sickness received the same concern and care as the misfortunes of a best friend. The response to a cry for help was never measured or limited by cost, danger, or discomfort to oneself. Olson's kind never looked at the price tag of an unselfish act or a mission of mercy. They simply gave to their utmost ability.

This, then, was the kind of man who received the serum from Seppala and headed west toward Nome at the height of a furious subarctic storm.

Olson waved good-by to Seppala at 3:15 Sunday afternoon and was immediately swallowed by the blizzard as he picked up the trail to Bluff. He answered the howling, icy wind with shouted words of encouragement to Jack, the leader of his seven-dog malamute team. Olson had checked the thermometer just before Seppala arrived at Golovin. It had registered 30° below zero. He estimated the wind at forty miles per hour and said a silent prayer that his dogs would be able to make the twenty-five miles to Bluff. They were rather short-haired for malamutes and therefore less protected from the freezing gale than heavier-coated dogs.

Olson wore his warmest trail clothes: reindeer boots, sealskin pants, and a double parka of ground squirrel, with a cotton snowshirt covering the fur. Inside the double fur hood he had a woolen cap pulled down over his ears. His mittens were dog skin, favored by many mushers for warmth and flexibility. Even with this protection, the freezing, biting wind quickly dissipated his body heat. No man with a knowledge of the North would have taken the trail in such severe weather unless it was a matter of life or death.

The gale had backed slightly to the north, and the wind was now blowing at right angles to the trail. As Olson came to Golovin Lagoon, a storm gust funneling through a valley of the low hills to his right struck him with hurricane force. The sled, the dogs, and Olson were lifted bodily and were hurled from the trail. When Olson fought his way to his feet, he found the sled half buried in a drift and the dogs hopelessly tangled in the harness. In the tempestuous darkness he calmly straightened out the snarled harness and drove on.

Charlie Olson drove the serum over twenty-five miles of the toughest section of the relay—from Golovin to Bluff—when the temperature fell to −30° and the wind reached hurricane force. This photograph was taken after the race. Two of the dogs shown here were replacements for dogs who were injured during the race.

A little later Olson felt the dogs were slowing down. He knew what this mean—they were freezing. He stopped, and with aching, ungloved hands fumbled for blankets in the sled. He carefully and methodically blanketed each dog in the team, knowing that while he was doing it, his hands were freezing. He shrugged off the thought that he might lose his fingers as of small importance compared with the suffering in Nome. As they continued westward, Olson and his team were blown from the trail time after time, but the musher drove stubbornly on.

As he struggled over slick ice and banks of drifted snow, he had visions of the roaring stove and hot coffee at the end of the trail. At 7:30 that evening his nearly frozen team, sensing the road-house a short distance ahead, tried painfully to quicken the pace.

Peering through the stinging, wind-whipped snow, Olson could make out a light. It was Bluff, and his roadhouse. The serum had traveled another painful step closer to its final goal, Nome, fifty-three miles away.

For years Olson had raced, bred, and sold sled dogs. His knowledge of dogs had helped him come through, but he had paid his debt to the storm; two of his favorite dogs were badly groin-frozen.

In the main room of Olson's Roadhouse at Bluff a rugged, six-foot-tall, 170-pound man hugged the warmth of the cherry-red Yukon stove while listening apprehensively to the clamoring, con-stantly changing voice of the storm raging outside.

Gunnar Kaasen wondered whether Charlie Olson had taken shelter in the blizzard or if he was trying to make it on through from Golovin. Kaasen had arrived the day before and had given Olson the message to drive his team to Golovin, to wait there for Seppala, and then to return to Bluff with the serum.

The big Norwegian had driven dog teams for twenty-one years in Alaska and understood the danger of a winter storm to an unprotected man and his team. Mushers he had known had frozen to death after becoming lost in the blinding, violent blizzards that without warning swept down from the arctic.

He had known one fortunate driver who owed his life to the superior canine sensory abilities and instinct of his lead dog. Lost, the musher had followed blindly, letting the leader pick his way until the man stumbled against a cabin hidden from human eyes in the storm.

It was now Sunday afternoon. He was still a little tired from his hurried fifty-three-mile trip from Nome and wondered whether he could chance a short nap, but decided he had better wait up for Olson. The minutes ticked slowly away. Kaasen went to the door from time to time and looked out into the wild, gray afternoon, but he could see nothing.

After he returned to his chair by the stove, he reached down and scratched the ears of a big black husky stretched out at his feet and who now thumped his tail against the floor in gratitude for the attention. Kaasen had sheltered his twelve other dogs in the roadhouse kennel, but he had allowed Balto, his lead dog, to come with him into the road-house. For some reason he could not explain clearly, he had always liked and trusted Balto.

Kaasen worked for the same mining company that employed Seppala. He knew that Seppala did not have a very high opinion of the big dog, although Seppala had named the dog after an admired fellow countryman, Lapp Baltow, who had accompanied Nansen on his exploration of Greenland in 1882. Still, Kaasen felt that he, too, was a good judge of dogs and that Seppala had missed something in the shaggy-coated husky with the distinctive white right foreleg.

Kaasen had been active in local races. But he felt that speed followed strength and ruggedness in the list of desirable attributes of a husky if the dog was to earn his living as a member of a working dog team. When Kaasen's boss, Summers, asked him to go to Bluff as a relay driver in the serum run, he unhesitatingly placed Balto in the lead position of

This formal portrait of Gunnar Kaasen and his lead dog, Balto, was taken shortly after the race to Nome.

the thirteen-dog freight team. Kaasen had confidence in the big dog. Perhaps the rugged musher identified with Balto in some way. They were not famous racers, man or dog, like Seppala and Togo, but they were both strong and steady.

The minutes turned into hours as Kaasen waited anxiously for Olson's arrival. Late in the afternoon Kaasen fed each of the dogs a whole dried salmon and a piece of tallow the size of his big fist. They would need the energy-giving food for the hard thirty-four-mile run to Pt. Safety, where Ed Rohn and his fast team were standing by at the roadhouse to make the final twenty-mile sprint into Nome. (The Rohn brothers' team had won every race they had entered in the preceding year.)

After feeding the dogs in the kennel, Kaasen went outside and looked down the trail to the east, hoping to see Olson. The wind was driving down the hills from the northwest and scouring the snow off the high places. The blowing snow felt like fine shot on his face, and he pulled his hood out further for protection. There was no sign of the roadhouse proprietor or his team, but Kaasen could see barely two hundred feet in the gathering darkness and storm.

By 7:30 Sunday night he estimated the wind had

risen to between forty and fifty miles per hour. Suddenly Balto growled, and his hackles rose. Above the screaming of the gale Kaasen heard a muffled shout. He pushed open the door of the primitive inn, and Charlie Olson staggered in.

"Gunnar," Olson said, "help me unlash the serum and bring my team in. I froze my fingers back on the trail blanketing my dogs. I'm afraid it didn't do any good; they're all moving like they're frozen in the groin. I don't think they could've gone another mile."

Kaasen went quickly to Olson's sled and unhitched the dogs from the towline and brought them into the warm cabin. The seven dogs walked stiffly and painfully; it was apparent they had suffered severely in the storm.

Olson pulled off his leather mittens and stood with his back to the stove, holding his hands away from the heat. His fingers were white with frostbite. He grimaced with pain as he flexed them slowly to restore the circulation. Olson would not lose them, but only those who have been frostbitten have known the burning, excruciating pain he would suffer in the days before the frozen flesh healed.

Finally Olson turned and slumped into a chair

close to the hot stove. "Gunnar," he said wearily, "let's take plenty of time to warm the serum. Perhaps the wind will go down in a few hours. I don't think you can make it through to Pt. Safety in this weather."

Olson told Kaasen that, as planned, he had picked up the serum from Seppala. "Seppala's team dropped in their tracks from exhaustion when they pulled into Golovin," Olson related. "Seppala told me that they had a hard trip across Norton Bay and along the coast from Isaac's Point."

Olson added that Seppala had used Togo and Scotty for leaders and that Seppala insisted that although his championship dogs were tired, they were still game.

Kaasen interrupted, "That Togo is a good dog. He knows what you want before you do."

Olson then told Kaasen about his own grueling twenty-five-mile mush from Golovin: How the wind was so violent it had blown the sled off the trail several times. Kaasen looked at his watch impatiently. Nearly two hours had passed since Olson's arrival, and if anything, the wind had increased. He looked at the thermometer outside the window of the cabin: It was −28°. The freezing effect of that temperature with a wind of over forty miles an hour could hardly be calculated.

The two men talked quietly for a while about conditions in Nome. Kaasen thought of Dr. Welch's tired, anxious face, of some of his friends in Nome who had contracted the disease, of the children who had already died.

He turned to Olson. "Charlie, there's no use waiting longer. If I don't go now, the trail between here and the Pt. Safety Roadhouse will have drifted so badly it will be impassable."

He walked out into the raging blizzard to the kennel and quickly hitched his dogs to the sled. The wind was fierce; he didn't know how hard it was blowing, but he had never experienced a stronger gale.

The big musher had dressed for the storm. He wore hip-length sealskin mukluks and sealskin pants over them. Over his head and shoulders to below his waist he wore a sealskin parka and hood, with a cotton drill parka over the fur jacket to blunt the wind and keep the snow from sticking to the fur. Even so, the icy blasts seemed to go right through to his skin.

He re-entered the roadhouse for the last time, picked up the twenty-pound package of serum, and said good-by to Olson.

XII END OF THE TRAIL

Fumbling in the darkness, Kaasen tied the precious package to the sled, careful to expose his hands for only a few seconds at a time. Finally it was done. He untied the snubline holding the team, and to a high-pitched yell, the dogs surged forward. They were glad, at first, for the warming exercise.

For a few miles along the coast Kaasen made good time. The wind had crusted the trail and there were few drifts. But five miles from Bluff, snow had drifted up in the lee of a ridge and the dogs floundered and sank to their bellies in the soft powder. Kaasen went forward to break trail for the stalled team, but in a few steps he was wallowing in snow to his chest. No, they could not make it. There was nothing to do but go back, circle the big drift and hope that in the darkness Balto would be able to pick up the snow-covered trail again.

He grasped Balto's harness, and the man's and dog's combined strength turned the team and led them from the deep snow.

Slowly and laboriously they probed their way around the ridge in the darkness, the dogs with their heads down as they struggled through the eddying snow. At last the team surged forward and Balto held a straight course. They were back on the trail.

A short time later the trail became flint-hard under foot. Through the swirling snow, black spots of wind-scoured ice told Kaasen they were crossing the Topkok River. As the team neared the west bank Balto stopped short. He looked back at Kaasen as the musher shouted impatiently for him to go on, but Balto did not budge. Kaasen walked forward to find out why his leader had balked. He was appalled to see Balto standing in a shallow overflow at a place where water had seeped up through a crack in the river ice. It could have been worse.

At least Balto had stopped in time to keep his teammates from entering the icy water.

The driver had to act fast; if he didn't, Balto's wet pads would stick to the glare ice and tear, and his feet would soon freeze. He quickly found a small snowdrift near the overflow. Kaasen then unhitched the big shaggy dog and led him to it. Balto instinctively worked his feet in the powdery snow to dry them. In a few minutes they were ready to start again.

"Gee, Balto!" Kaasen yelled, and the big dog swung the team right, leading them again into a lope that left the treacherous overflow a safe distance to the south.

Suddenly, in the storm, a dark mass loomed ahead. It was Topkok Hill. Mushers dreaded the exposed six-hundred-foot summit in any but the mildest weather. On this night Kaasen knew what to expect of the barren, steep hill overlooking the Bering Sea. He grimly braced himself for the ascent as he shouted words of encouragement to the dogs.

He was breathing heavily from the exertion of pushing the sled uphill to help the team over the steep grade, and the wind knifing down the slope chilled him to the bone. Halfway up Topkok his

Gunnar Kaasen knew that Balto, his favorite dog, was not as fast and clever as Seppala's Togo. But he felt Balto's ruggedness and steady temperament were just as important as Togo's outstanding qualities. This photograph was taken during a pause in one of Kaasen's winter journeys. Note the hoar frost on his hood.

right cheek, which had been burning and aching from the biting northwest wind, became numb. He rubbed it with his mittened hand, but there was no feeling. It was frozen. "This place is hell when it storms, but we'll make it," he shouted defiantly into the wind. The big man and his thirteen dogs fought on to the summit. Suddenly they were racing downward in the darkness, victorious over another obstacle on the trail to Nome.

From the bottom of the hill the trail continued across a six-mile flat stretch on the way to the Solomon Roadhouse, thirteen miles distant. The dogs seemed to fly over the even, wind-crusted snow. The wind dropped gradually, and until Kaasen reached Spruce Creek, seven miles from Solomon, it seemed as if the elements were beginning to take pity on the man and his dog team.

But at Spruce Creek the wind again struck Kaasen with demoniacal force. Blowing snow became so dense that at times the musher could not see his wheel dog. Mile after mile he drove on without being able to see the trail. It seemed improbable that Balto could find his way across the glare ice of the many lagoons along the coast, but Kaasen had no choice but to follow blindly and trust his leader.

At the height of the storm, as Kaasen mushed westward, the Board of Health in Nome telephoned a message to Solomon, the eastern end of the telephone line from Nome. The board felt that the storm was so severe the lives of the mushers carrying the serum would be endangered if they drove on through it. The message for Kaasen instructed him to wait at Solomon for the weather to moderate before continuing on to Pt. Safety. Shortly after the phone call was received, the telephone wires went down in the storm, severing further communication.

As the miles slipped by in the darkness and storm, Kaasen did not know that he had finally reached Solomon. The trail passed to the south of the little settlement, and Balto continued relentlessly on toward Nome. It was not until two miles farther on that Kaasen recognized the outlines of Bonanza Slough during a lull in the storm. He realized then they had passed by Solomon without seeing it. He had no way of knowing of the board's instructions to wait out the storm.

Crossing Bonanza flats, a strong gust of wind struck Kaasen and the team. He was unable to prevent the sled from being flipped over, pulling some

This photograph of Kaasen and his team gives an accurate impression of the way they looked during the race toward Nome, except for differences in the time of day and the weather conditions.

of the dogs down with it. When the gust had spent itself, the musher righted the sled and untangled the dogs. Before starting again, he felt in the sled to make sure the serum was still securely lashed in place. At first, as he groped in the bottom of the sled, he refused to believe his searching hands.

Then, as the terrible realization came to him, he was seized by a heavy sinking feeling in the pit of his stomach: The twenty-pound package was gone! He dropped to his hands and knees and searched frantically in the snow where the sled had capsized. It was too dark to see; he would have to find it by touch.

Thoughts that nearly made him physically sick raced through his mind—perhaps he had lost the serum farther back on the trail. It would be covered with snow by now and impossible to find. He pulled off his mittens and groped through cold snow with his bare hands. After the serum had traveled over six hundred miles and was almost at its destination, was he to be the one who failed?

In the darkness his right hand bumped something, and he gave an involuntary shout. Relief flooded slowly over him as he lifted the package of antitoxin from the snow and retied it carefully to the sled.

After crossing Bonanza, the trail swung south-west and the wind veered to the north. Kaasen now had a quartering wind at his back. The team flew over the trail, covering the next twelve miles in eighty minutes. Kaasen reached Pt. Safety some time after two o'clock Sunday morning. The wind was dropping rapidly, and it was only twenty-one miles to Nome.

The cabin at Pt. Safety was dark. Ed Rohn was asleep. He had gone to bed thinking Kaasen had received the board's message instructing him to wait in Solomon until the blizzard blew itself out. Rohn did not expect Kaasen before daylight.

Outside in the darkness Kaasen deliberated whether to wake Ed Rohn, whom the board had asked to make the final sprint to Nome. He was tired, but the worst of the trip was over. His dogs had suffered, but were still going well, although two who had been frozen on an earlier trip showed signs of stiffness. Other thoughts flashed through his mind, but in the end were crowded out by a growing determination. No, he would not wake Rohn and delay the delivery of the serum while Ed Rohn dressed and harnessed his dogs. He, Kaasen, would finish the last leg of the serum race to Nome. He skirted the Pt. Safety Roadhouse, and Balto

Dr. Welch and Gunnar Kaasen posed for this picture showing the delivery of the antitoxin to the doorway of the hospital. When Kaasen actually arrived, most of the townspeople were still in bed; and those at the hospital were much too anxious to have thought of taking pictures. Note that the package in this photograph is square instead of cylindrical, as was the real package of serum.

COURTESY OF MRS. CURTIS WELCH

once again headed west. (Kaasen's decision to by-pass Ed Rohn was the cause of a controversy that has lasted through the years and cast a shadow over the heroic serum drive. The claims and counter-claims as to why Kaasen passed Pt. Safety are set forth in the Epilogue.)

The trail from Pt. Safety to Nome followed the beach. Snow had drifted heavily in places between ice hummocks on the frozen sea and the upper beach, but Balto ploughed through them. A few miles on from Pt. Safety, Kaasen stopped and put rabbit-skin covers on the two dogs showing signs of soreness.

The last miles to Nome seemed interminable to the leaden-legged man. Finally a few yellow lights flickered in the murky distance. The tired driver shouted words of encouragement to his exhausted dogs, and seeming to understand that the trip was nearly over, they trotted a little faster.

At 5:30 Monday morning, Kaasen swung up from the beach and onto Nome's deserted Front Street. Most of the town was still sleeping. No one expected the serum to come through the blizzard. Only a few early risers saw Kaasen and his team enter Nome.

Dr. Welch was awakened by a persistent knocking at his front door. He opened it and was handed a fur-and-canvas-covered twenty-pound package by a man who swayed and almost fell. In the street thirteen dogs harnessed to a sled stood quietly. Their heads and bushy tails hung almost to the ground. They had covered the last bitter fifty-three miles of the epic race in seven and a half hours.

These dogs, and other dogs like these behind them, had traversed 674 ice-and-snow-covered miles in one hundred and twenty-seven and a half hours—in less than five and a half days—to bring Nome the antitoxin, the life-saving serum that in less than a week would break the back of the diphtheria epidemic.

EPILOGUE

When Dr. Welch opened the serum package, he found the entire 300,000 units solidly frozen. For a moment, the doctor's soaring hopes were dashed, but a radiogram to the U.S. Public Health Service brought immediate reassurance. Nome's invisible enemy had not won a reprieve; the antitoxin was unharmed by the freezing.

Dr. G. M. Magruder, director in Seattle, replied to Dr. Welch that experts at the H. K. Mulford Company, the manufacturers of the serum, as well as those of Eli Lilly and Abbott laboratories, said the efficacy of the serum had not been jeopardized, if it was thawed carefully. By noon on February 2, 1925, Dr. Welch was inoculating the ill with the life-saving liquid. Using the first batch in small doses to cure early cases and prevent infection of the exposed, the epidemic was broken. There were no further deaths, and by February 21, Nome's general quarantine was lifted. It had been in effect exactly a month.

After the epidemic ended, Dr. and Mrs. Welch were discussing possible causes of the outbreak of the disease. Suddenly Mrs. Welch recalled that in November a native family arrived in Nome by sled from Holy Cross on the Yukon via St. Michael, and one of the children had died the following day. The mother told the doctor the infant had cold symptoms, but she felt the long hard trip had been responsible for its death. The doctor and Lula Welch concurred that in all probability this family had been the carrier of the diphtheria bacillus.

Five days after Gunnar Kaasen had delivered the serum to Dr. Welch, the second batch of 1,100,000 units arrived in Seward, Alaska, aboard the S.S. *Alameda* and was shipped in record time by a special train to Nenana. From there, this serum again was transported across Alaska by dog teams. Many of the same drivers and teams that carried the first

300,000 units of serum participated in the second run as far as Unalakleet, but over different sections of the same trail. Unfortunately there were a few new drivers in the second drive who were never given public recognition for their courageous efforts.

Once again the mushers made remarkable time, and the only records available show that they made the 456-mile trip to Unalakleet in eighty hours. The temperatures for the first part of the trip were even more severe than those on the earlier serum drive. During the run the mercury registered $-54°$ at Nenana, $-58°$ at Manley Hot Springs, and $-50°$ at Tanana. At Ruby the temperature was $-30°$, but was compounded by a strong wind.

After the serum race each of the drivers was given a donation of $18.66 from a public subscription fund, as well as $25 a day by the Territory for the time they were involved. Most of the men received between $30 and $40. Governor Scott Bone issued the drivers a parchment citation with the territorial gold seal, praising their heroism. The H. K. Mulford Company sent inscribed medals to the drivers of the first relay and awarded Gunnar Kaasen $1,000 for his part in the serum race.

The serum race was over, but reverberations

from the dramatic event—some good, some bad—continued for years.

Nome's diphtheria epidemic focused the nation's attention on the virulent disease. Until 1925 there were some 210,000 cases and 20,000 diphtheria deaths annually in the United States. Publicity given the event brought about widespread inoculation. In a short time the diphtheria bacillus was relegated to a minor position on the nation's roster of dread diseases.

The day after the serum arrived in Nome, the Associated Press, under a Washington dateline, reported the epidemic had spurred the Post Office Department into immediate plans for airmail service in Alaska.

Everywhere in remote areas, known antitoxins were stockpiled against emergencies such as Nome's.

But for some the serum drive created controversy, jealousy, and lifelong enmities. Gunnar Kaasen's decision to bypass Ed Rohn at Pt. Safety started a feud that still sputters.

Ed Rohn, Leonhard Seppala, and many others in Nome at the time felt that Kaasen had purposely bypassed Rohn at Pt. Safety in order to get the lion's share of the publicity as the finishing team.

Kaasen's accusers point out that by the time he left Nome for Golovin, he was well aware the epic race had captured the world's attention. The Signal Corps wireless office in Nome was processing many queries daily from the national and international press.

To corroborate their contention of Kaasen's duplicity, the anti-Kaasen faction has assembled miscellaneous evidence. A month after the event, Peter Curran at the roadhouse in Solomon, in answer to an inquiry of Mrs. Seppala's, said there was "little wind" when Kaasen passed Solomon, and the next morning he found his sled tracks thirty-five feet from the cabin.

Mr. Seppala states that Kaasen had an agreement with a Charlie Dahlquist at the Pt. Safety Road-house to have a light in the upper window if there was another relay team waiting there when Kaasen passed. He added that when Kaasen saw the light in the window he left the trail and detoured out over the frozen lagoon away from the roadhouse so the Rohn dogs would not hear the Kaasen team and give the alarm.

The Kaasen supporters accept his version that the Pt. Safety Roadhouse was dark when he arrived

COURTESY OF NEW YORK CITY PARK DEPARTMENT

This bronze statue of Balto is a familiar sight to visitors to New York's Central Park. Although some Alaskans believe that Leonhard Seppala's Togo was more deserving of the honor, the memorial still pays fitting tribute to the "Endurance, Fidelity, Intelligence" of all twenty dog teams that participated in the race.

and that he did not wish to delay the final twenty-one-mile drive to Nome by waiting for Rohn to dress and harness his dogs. Kaasen's more ardent backers state he would have made a mistake if he had turned the serum over to Rohn, as Rohn and his team were inexperienced in mushing under severe weather conditions.

The story was further clouded by distorted and highly colored news accounts of the episode.

Kaasen's award of $1,000 from the H. K. Mulford Company added more fuel to the fire, and later offers made him by a moving picture company to act and stateside vaudeville offers to appear with his finishing team did nothing to placate the disgruntled.

Mr. Seppala repeatedly brought up the point that he was the first man chosen to pick up the serum, and that the original plan was to send him all the way to Nulato. No one seemed concerned that the tough little Indians and a few whites along the Yukon who carried the serum over two-thirds of the way were forgotten men in the great race.

Seppala was further embittered when Balto was chosen by the press as the canine hero of the event, and was righteously outraged when Togo's race records were mistakenly attributed to Balto. The final, crushing blow for Seppala came when Balto, instead of his favorite Togo, was immortalized with the casting of a bronze statue of the big black dog for New York City's Central Park.

Whatever the claims and counter-claims have been, it would seem that the men involved in the controversy lost track of one all-important fact: The serum was successfully and safely carried over 674 miles of difficult trail in remarkable time by men of great endurance and their tough, courageous dogs.

Balto became a symbol of the heroic northern sled dog who participated in the memorable drive. To the American public the glorified husky was representative of Jack, Dixie, Togo, and every other leader and dog that helped carry the antitoxin and hope to the people of Nome.

The inscription on the base of Balto's statue, "Endurance, Fidelity, Intelligence," seems a fitting tribute to an ordinary husky who, when the chips were down, came through against heavy odds, and to all his canine brothers in the great serum race, who were truly man's best friends in the winter of 1925.

CHRONOLOGY OF THE SERUM RACE

January 27–28 "Wild Bill" Shannon—Nenana to Tolovana (52 miles)

28 Dan Green—Tolovana to Manley Hot Springs (31 miles)

28 Johnny Folger—Manley Hot Springs to Fish Lake (28 miles)

29 Sam Joseph—Fish Lake to Tanana (26 miles)

29 Titus Nikoli—Tanana to Kallands (34 miles)

29 Dave Corning—Kallands to Nine Mile mail cabin (24 miles)

29 Edgar Kalland—Nine Mile to Kokrines (30 miles)

29 Harry Pitka—Kokrines to Ruby (30 miles)

29 Bill McCarty—Ruby to Whiskey Creek (28 miles)

29–30 Edgar Nollner—Whiskey Creek to Galena (24 miles)

30 George Nollner—Galena to Bishop Mountain (18 miles)

30 Charlie Evans—Bishop Mountain to Nulato (30 miles)

30 Tommy Patsy—Nulato to Kaltag (36 miles)

30 Jackscrew—Kaltag to Old Woman shelter house (40 miles)

30–31 Victor Anagick—Old Woman to Unalakleet (34 miles)

31 Myles Gonangnan—Unalakleet to Shaktolik (40 miles)

31 Henry Ivanoff—starts from Shaktolik to Golovin but meets Seppala, who takes the run

31–
February 1 Leonhard Seppala—Shaktolik to Golovin (91 miles)

1 Charlie Olson—Golovin to Bluff (25 miles)

1–2 Gunnar Kaasen—Bluff to Nome (53 miles)

TOTAL MILES: 674
TOTAL TIME: 127½ hours

(The mileage of the race and mail trail has been given in early records as from 658 to 683 miles. The mileage in this chronology is based upon records checked against the statements of the surviving drivers.)

INDEX

[Figures in boldface indicate pages upon which illustrations appear.]

167